Never Finished . . .

NEWTON R~~...~~t Begun

Never Finished . . . Just Begun

A Narrative History of L. B. Sharp and Outdoor Education

by Julie Carlson

Beaver's Pond Press, Inc.

Edina, Minnesota

ISBN 10: 1-59298-249-2
ISBN 13: 978-1-59298-249-3

Library of Congress Control Number: 2008932317
Printed in the United States of America
First Printing: 2009
12 11 10 09   6 5 4 3 2 1

Cover and interior design by Clay Schotzko
Photos pages vi, 92, 120, 143, 152 courtesy Donald Rettew
Photo page 14 courtesy Geneva McKenzie
Photos pages 17, 24, 47, 146 photographer unknown
Photo page 21 Julie Carlson
Photos page 57, 69, 111 courtesy the Outdoor Education Association, Inc.
Photo page 85 courtesy New York University
Photo page 129 courtesy Frank Gunnell

Beaver's Pond Press, Inc.

Beaver's Pond Press is an imprint of
Beaver's Pond Group
7104 Ohms Lane
Edina, MN 55439-2129
(952) 829-8818
www.BeaversPondPress.com

To order, visit www.BookHouseFulfillment.com
or call (800) 901-3480. Reseller discounts available.

*This book is lovingly dedicated to
Mary Lou, Ronald, Matthew, and Skyler*

Table of Contents

Foreword. 1

Preface. 3

Introduction. 9

Chapter 1: The Early Years (1895–1925) 15

Chapter 2: The Middle Years (1925–1940): Launching of a Career . . . 25

Chapter 3: Growth of the Movement (1940s). 55

Chapter 4: Endings and New Beginnings (1950s) 73

Chapter 5: Relocation to Southern Illinois University (1959–1963). . 93

Chapter 6: The Passing of Lloyd Burgess Sharp (1963 and Beyond). . . 103

Chapter 7: L. B.'s Leadership 117

Chapter 8: Epilogue. 147

Appendix A: About the Narrators 153

Appendix B: Heart-of-the-Hills View Poem. 163

Appendix C: Millard van Dien Poem. 165

References 167

Foreword

Dr. L. B. Sharp's impact on people, education, and the outdoors has been captured exquisitely in this work by Dr. Julie Carlson. She masterfully probed the minds of nine renowned outdoor educators who knew Sharp over a period of years. They reflected on his extraordinary influence on them and their professional lives as well as the outdoor education movement from its inception. Sharp's life is re-kindled through personal reflections and archival materials from a variety of sources that Dr. Carlson wove together in a very readable fashion. This book is an important read for teachers, school and camp administrators, students, and everyone interested in leadership and in outdoor education in its many manifestations.

While my time with Dr. Sharp was very limited, he nevertheless greatly influenced me and my university teaching as well as my early work with teachers, principals, and other educational administrators in creating the school outdoor education program in Rockford, Illinois, in the late 1950s. At a conference at Camp Reinberg near Palatine, Illinois, I showed Dr. Sharp plans for a new outdoor education center that the Rockford Park District was going to build for multi-uses including resident outdoor education. Sharp was critical of the plans for the Atwood Outdoor Education Center for not being decentralized. Budget constraints and limited understanding by the Rockford Park District Board of Directors were obstacles that had to be overcome to be able to build one building, not to mention several as Dr. Sharp's philosophy, and mine, dictated. The facility continues operating to this day, over 45 years later, with resident outdoor education programs for Rockford area schools and schools as far away as Chicago.

I found it to be most enjoyable reading comments by all of the outstanding outdoor education leaders in this study of the life of Dr. L. B. Sharp. A time with two of them came to mind. I couldn't help but visualize Tom Rillo, Cliff Knapp, and me sitting in a motel hot tub in Champaign, Illinois, about 15 years ago. We were the Lloyd B. Sharp Award committee deciding on the next recipient of that national recognition. The three of us had received the award in previous years. I think L. B. would have preferred that we held our meeting by a lake or stream in the woods somewhere. It was a privilege to help to preserve the memory of one who so greatly impacted education and leadership as Dr. Carlson has done in this book.

Dr. Frank Lupton

Preface

[L. B. Sharp] was recognized as "The Chief" because he was the originator, the promoter, and the chief authority in his own special segment of the field of education. He was an educator, and was one of the important figures in educational change in the United States in his lifetime. (Conrad, 1972, p. 16)

It would seem to me that a research-minded individual would make a worthy contribution by interviewing those who associated with L. B. and asking penetrating questions. A biographer might set forth why L. B. did those things that mean so much to others. (Vinal, 1972, p. 47)

Long before discovering Dr. William (Cap'n Bill) Vinal's quote above, I had developed a deep intrigue for Lloyd Burgess Sharp, affectionately known as "L. B." to his friends and associates. I first became introduced to Sharp during my undergraduate studies by a special professor and mentor, Bonnie Black, at Central Michigan University. My minor discipline of study was in outdoor education. I found a congruence of Sharp's philosophy of education with that of my own, albeit mine was very much in a developmental infancy at the time. Later, while completing teacher certification coursework, I discovered my views were also strongly aligned with the writings of American philosopher and educator John Dewey.

It was not until some additional years had passed, however, when I was casually leafing through an old issue of *Camping* magazine, that my eyes landed on something that caused me to bolt upright in my chair. A single line mentioned that L. B. Sharp had been a doctoral student studying under John Dewey at Columbia University. A sudden harmonic convergence of sorts, that one line of text connecting Sharp with Dewey sparked the kindling for this study and has kept it fueled ever since. I have come to believe that Sharp's original premise or thesis of outdoor education represents one of the most successful applications of Deweyan pragmatic educational philosophy yet to be revealed:

> That which can best be learned inside the classroom should be learned there. That which can best be learned in the out-of-doors through direct experience, dealing with native materials and life situations, should there be learned. (Sharp, 1943a, p. 363–364)

Upon beginning disciplined inquiry into Sharp's career, I examined significant amounts of information regarding Sharp and his influence on the history and current status of outdoor education. I was able to piece together events and actions that led to the evolution of outdoor education through its early beginnings in school outings, camping education, school camping, and eventually to outdoor education. Still, I found myself yearning for more. Who was he as a person? What was it that led him to do what he did? How did he carry himself ethically and morally? What beliefs did he hold? What was his leadership style? Why did people listen to him, and follow him? Why did they try to copy what he was doing? How was it that this one person was able to foster such an admirable cadre of other influential leaders of various genres of experiential education such as outdoor, adventure, environmental, conservation, wilderness, holistic, and therapeutic?

These important pieces of information were missing from the literature or existed in small, incomplete chunks. The written narrative descriptions of Sharp that I located, such as those by Knapp (2000), Rillo (1980a), and Vinal (1972), offer insightful glimpses into his character. Partial biographical sketches were found in the form of chronological listings of events as parts of larger studies by dissertation researchers such as Fine (1987), Piercy (1978), and Wiener (1965). Although these pieces of literature are meaningful and relevant, they are short in scope and length in terms of Sharp's career. A lengthy narrative that presented an in-depth history of Sharp's career history did not exist. An extensive study would offer insight into the life of Sharp, his career, and the formation of the entire approach to learning known as outdoor education. Furthermore, discovering who he was and how he influenced others who became educational leaders in their own right would add to the continually evolving body of research literature on leadership, a passionate topic of interest for me.

Conceptual Framework of the Research

Reflecting on William Vinal's suggestion that it would be a worthy endeavor to find out why the things that L. B. did were so meaningful to those who were associated with him, it made sense that people who knew Sharp would be the most knowledgeable in answering my questions about him. With the help of renowned educator Dr. Clifford Knapp, recently retired from Northern Illinois University and also a former student and colleague of Sharp, I obtained the names of several living persons who had been Sharp's associates. Some of these people knew Sharp as collegial professors or as professional outdoor educators. Some of them were students of Sharp who later became his colleagues. Most of them had publications that could be found in the literature on outdoor education. Additionally, I was aware that Southern Illinois University in Carbondale held an extensive collection of the life works of L. B. Sharp in the university's Morris Library - Special Collections.

I determined that the most appropriate method to answer my questions surrounding Sharp as a person and leader was a life history approach, meaning an interpretation of historical events that is partially constructed through narratives gathered from those who experienced the events (Ritchie, 1995). A life history focuses on a life with several significant events shaping that life (Hatch & Wisniewski, 1995). Life histories also contain corroborative archival data. This career history resulted in the construction of a narrative-based interpretation of historical events in relation to Sharp's life. Narrative data were collected through interviews held during 2001 and 2002 with nine people who had been associates of Sharp (see Appendix A for names and descriptions of the narrators). The interviews were audio-recorded and transcribed. The narrators then were given the opportunity to "member-check" their transcripts for accuracy. The narrative data were triangulated with archival data collected from the Morris Library - Special Collections and other sources. Both narrative and archival data were then merged into a chronological interpretive text or storyline (Polkinghorne, 1995) in presenting Sharp's career history. For the identification of emergent themes in Sharp's approach to leadership, qualitative analysis procedures proposed by Strauss and Corbin (1998) were used.

Acknowledgements

I have many people to thank for their assistance and support throughout the research and writing process. As mentioned earlier, Clifford Knapp provided my "place to start" by providing connections to the people who became narrators for the study. He has also provided photographs, artifacts, and reviewed various sections of text I've written regarding L. B. Sharp. His enthusiasm and support in turning the study into book form has remained constant through the years. It is accurate to say that this study would not have taken place without him.

Countless others I met along the way were relatives or admirers of L. B. They enthusiastically shared their stories, insights, and artifacts. I thank them all for their contributions. Specific gratitude goes to Alma Taylor, Judith Carpenter, Curt Carter, Elizabeth Weir, Frank Lupton, and Paul Yambert. Katie Salzman at the Morris Library at Southern Illinois University and Margaret Hawley of the Osage County Historical Association in Kansas were patient and helpful. Charles McFatridge and Evelyn Rhodes volunteered hours of proofreading and editing. Larry Hickman and Rebecca Sharpless willingly reviewed specific content on the philosophy of John Dewey and on oral-life history methodology, respectively. This study began as a dissertation study, and I still to this day deeply appreciate the time and guidance that my committee members offered: Betty Alford, Karen Mayo, Patsy Hallman, and Garth Petrie. Thanks goes also to my colleagues and dean at my current place of employment, Minnesota State University at Mankato, for providing release time and travel funding to continue research for the study.

In addition to proofreading the original text, the interest and support of my parents has been motivational. My loving thanks goes to them for influencing my professional and personal pathways in education, the outdoors, and in trying to make the world a better place. Deep love and gratitude goes to my life partner, Matthew, who said, "Get 'er done!" and daughter, Skyler, who makes it all worth it as I watch her love and wonder of the outdoors continue to blossom.

The folks at Beaver's Pond Press have been respectfully patient and supportive through the entire publishing process. There have been many involved, but special recognition goes to my managing editor, Dara Moore, for her cheerful direction, and to Clay Schotzko for his remarkable talents in capturing L. B. Sharp's life and spirit in the design of the book cover and interior.

And of course, the bright shining stars of the study were the narrators: Ed Ambry, Bob Christie, Elizabeth Roller, Ellie Morrison, Tom Rillo, Cliff Knapp, Larry Huntley, Don Hammerman, and Clifford Emanuelson. I am humbled by their openness, willingness, and enthusiasm to share their stories without hesitation. Not only do I thank them for their help in bringing the legacy of L. B. to the public eye, I thank them for their own contributions in bringing the outdoors to hundreds of thousands of people throughout their own careers in outdoor education. The love for the outdoors and the planet Earth that they have helped to instill will, without question, aid us all in our motivation and drive to find solutions as global environmental concerns continue to rise.

Introduction

During the late 1920s, Lloyd Burgess Sharp (1895–1963) was a doctoral student at Teachers College - Columbia University in New York. While studying there, he embraced the educational philosophy of a group of Columbia professors known as the "New Educators" (Rillo, 1980a). This group included John Dewey, William H. Kilpatrick, E. L. Thorndike, E. K. Fretwell, and others (Hammerman, et al., 1994). As an outdoor leader by profession, Sharp experimented with integrating the pragmatic and progressive philosophies of the New Educators, especially those of John Dewey, with the youth camping programs with which he was involved. Practical, hands-on, sensory-oriented, and experiential-learning experiences in small cooperative groups were components of Dewey's philosophy that Sharp implemented to teach traditional school subjects in outdoor settings (Rillo, 1980a). This intersection of New Education with outdoor learning situations resulted in a slow, but continual, formation of an approach to learning that eventually came to be known as *outdoor education*. Its period of greatest growth in use and popularity, generally from the mid-1940s through the 1970s, has often been described as the *outdoor education movement* (Hammerman & Hammerman, 1980).

During his career, Sharp held administrative, faculty, and consultant positions in various arenas of outdoor education. During his involvement with *Life* magazine's Fresh Air Camps, Sharp restructured the programs and facilities to provide outdoor educative experiences for inner-city youth in the northeastern United States. Later, through his establishment of National Camp and partnership with New York University, he also created outdoor leadership-preparation programs for teachers (Hammerman & Hammerman, 1980). He served as a faculty member at New York University, Columbia University, the Lab School at the University of Chicago, and Southern Illinois University. At the time of his death in 1963, he was both a professor emeritus at Southern Illinois University and the executive director of the Outdoor Education Association that was headquartered there (Wiener, 1965).

In conjunction with his other positions of employment, Sharp was an outdoor education consultant. He designed over 100 outdoor education facilities in the United States. For many of those, he personally served as the director of the construction projects. Additionally, he was hired as a curriculum consultant for countless outdoor education programs (Fine, 1987). Most of these facilities and programs still operate today.

Sharp published extensively on his philosophy of outdoor education, and he conducted a seminal research study with the New York City Public Schools revealing the educational outcomes of outdoor learning experiences in comparison to indoor classroom learning experiences. Although there were numerous outdoor leaders and educators who were involved in the formative years of outdoor education, L. B. Sharp was the "pioneer" (Rillo, 1994, p. xiv) who experimented with John Dewey's philosophy in outdoor settings and first coined the term *outdoor education* (Knapp, 2000). L. B. Sharp is often referred to as the Father of Outdoor Education (Beckett, 1963; Rillo, 1980a; Wiener, 1965).

The Influence of John Dewey

A particular significance of Sharp's shaping of the outdoor education movement was the integration of pragmatic and progressive philosophies of education, especially those of American philosopher John Dewey, with outdoor experiences. Dewey described knowledge, or knowing, as the combination of experience and cognition, and he therefore stressed "the early interrelation of manual discipline and intellectual discipline" (Brumbaugh & Lawrence, 1963, p. 126). Dewey (1916/1997a) claimed, "It is only in experience that any theory has vital and verifiable significance" (p. 144). Dewey believed in a pragmatic approach of using direct educative experiences, sometimes in the outdoors, when such experiences were the most appropriate way to learn the subject at hand. In describing the ideal home and school, Dewey (1900/1990) posited, "The life of the child would extend out of doors to the garden, surrounding fields, and forests. He would have his excursions, his walks and talks, in which the larger world out of doors would open to him" (p. 35).

Dewey (1937) expressed his concern that "the average American child seldom comes in direct contact with Nature. . . . He is in danger of losing contact with primitive realities: with the world, with the space about him, with fields and rivers, with the problems of getting shelter and obtaining food that have always conditioned human life and that still do so." Dewey used the term *nature study* to designate learning in and about the outdoors. He often included nature study in his discussions of what he felt direct experiences and curricula should include. He emphasized, "We cannot overlook the importance for educational purposes of the close and intimate acquaintance got with nature at first hand, with real things and materials, with the actual processes of their manipulation, and the knowledge of their social necessities and uses" (Dewey, 1900/1990, p. 11).

In addition to these beliefs about direct experiences, Dewey (1938/1997b) encouraged democratic learning, cooperative learning, constructivist learning, and hands-on learning. He proposed that schools should be miniature communities and should serve as "a genuine form of active community life, instead of a place set apart in which to learn lessons" (Dewey, 1900/1990, p. 14). Outdoor education, especially when used in residential settings, admirably implements these types of learning by involving students in group decision-making, group living, and learning and applying new outdoor knowledge and skills.

Well beyond influencing Sharp and outdoor education, Dewey is widely recognized as significantly shaping educational thought in America (Hickman, 1998). According to Hickman, Dewey "is now generally recognized as one of the seminal thinkers of the twentieth century" (p. ix). Brumbaugh and Lawrence (1963) claimed, "Plato alone competes with Dewey for having shaped contemporary civilization educationally" (p. 125). Clandinin and Connelly (2000) attributed much of their philosophy of qualitative research and narrative inquiry to Dewey. Although others molded their thinking over time, they explained, "Dewey's writings on the nature of experience remained our conceptual, imaginative backdrop" (p. 2). They described him as "the preeminent thinker in education" (p. 2). In describing Dewey's ongoing influence, Hickman (1998) offered,

> Today, John Dewey's work is once again in the forefront of American philosophy. Its contributions to environmental studies, feminist studies, multicultural studies, and even cognitive science are the subject of ongoing investigation by a new generation of philosophers. (p. xii)

Significance of the Study

This study is significant for its addition of evidence of the continual and extensive influence of Dewey on American education. However, beyond perpetuating Deweyan philosophy, outdoor education holds an admirable place in history and education on its own. By the 1980s, the use of outdoor education had spread to the point of being described as a movement (Hammerman & Hammerman, 1980). Outdoor education has grown from a few scattered experimental projects in the early 1900s to thousands of varied programs and facilities across the country and around the world. Outdoor education approaches have been intermingled with environmental and adventure-oriented approaches to learning (Hammerman et al., 1994).

Outdoor education is being implemented by schools, camps, youth agencies, corporate groups, churches, and other nonprofit and for-profit organizations. Programs are offered for all age levels from infants to adults. Outdoor education experiences take place in such varied settings as schoolyards, camps, farms, parks, living history museums, zoos, cemeteries, wilderness areas, aquatic areas, and urban neighborhoods (Hammerman et al., 1994). Outdoor education programs can be implemented through day or residential programs. Lessons using outdoor education approaches can span five minutes or several weeks of time.

The information provided by this study informs the practice of educators in all realms of experiential and traditional education. Educators will benefit through their understanding of the history of outdoor education and L. B. Sharp's role in shaping this approach to learning. This study contributes to the history of outdoor education, an approach to learning that holds a documentable place in the history of American education. Through inquiry into Sharp's approach to leadership, this study further affirms current perspectives that personal attributes of individual leaders beyond knowledge and technical skills are necessary to be inspirational and transformational leaders. A case is made for leaders whose competence includes qualities that foster admiration, trust, and a desire to follow.

— 1 —

The Early Years (1895–1925)

Growing up in Kansas

L. B. Sharp's parents were John Newton Sharp and Emma Ann Stucker Sharp ("Death certificate," 1963). John's boyhood years were spent in Whitehouse, New Jersey. It is not known how Emma and John came to meet, but they married in 1882 in Millersburg, Ohio, which was Emma's home state. In 1884, after one year of living in Fredericksburg, Ohio, the young couple journeyed west and settled on a farm on the outskirts of Carbondale, Kansas, where they would live the remainder of their married years. For the family's first 20 years in Kansas, John worked in the real estate and insurance business. He then served 18 years as a rural mail carrier in the Carbondale area. News clippings and other documentation collected through the Osage County Historical Society in Kansas reveal that John was involved in many community and civic endeavors, including serving 12 years on the local board of education. He was appreciative of music, both vocal and instrumental, and he helped to organize a community orchestra in Carbondale ("John N. Sharp," 1924).

Somewhat less information is documented regarding Emma, who was born in Fredericksburg, Ohio. She was a public school teacher for several years before she was married. Once the Sharps moved to Kansas, Emma was active in community affairs and volunteered with the local public schools ("Mrs. Emma Sharp dead," 1930).

L. B. was born on the Carbondale family farm on March 22, 1895 ("Lloyd B. Sharp," 1963), the youngest of four children (Wiener, 1965). He had an older sister Ruth, and two older brothers, Allen and Newton ("John N. Sharp," 1924). The following narratives provide insight into Sharp's upbringing on the farm in Kansas.

> He came from a farming family. His father was a farmer. . . . He came from a very poor family. . . . He had a father that was not a very energetic farmer, so a lot of the farming went to . . . a couple of other brothers. He was the youngest one. They took over the farm. His father became a mailman (E. Ambry, personal communication, February 10, 2002).

> That rural experience of growing up on a farm, I think, was one of his very early outdoor influences (T. Rillo, personal communication, December 27, 2001).

Farm life. L. B. has been described by many as an engaging and purposive storyteller who apparently enjoyed embellishing the same stories repeatedly. The following few stories describe life on the Carbondale farm and reveal stories the narrators had heard enough times to be able to retell themselves with vivid recall:

> It was his job to shut up the chickens at night. He would individually push them in, and herd them into these chicken houses. . . . He had the bright idea that he would weigh the doors down with a weight and trigger them off all at once. He would sprinkle seed to get them in, and they would get in by following the seed. . . . Once they were all in, he would pull this lever and all the doors would shut. But unfortunately, every once in a while, a chicken wouldn't be completely inside. It would be part way in, and the door, of course, would get it, and it would probably die, either by being crushed or

by suffocation. Mrs. Sharp, L. B.'s mother, would say to her husband, 'Have you noticed that we have fewer chickens than we had last week?' A week later, there would be even fewer chickens. The chicken flock was diminishing. So, probably his father said, 'I'll go out and see Bob,'—they called him Bob—'and see what he is doing out there.' That's [when his father] found out what he was doing experimentally. L. B. Sharp said, 'That was the end of my first effort at creativity' (T. Rillo, personal communication, December 27, 2001).

Another time, it was L. B.'s job to bring the hay from up above for the livestock, the cows, the horses, and the mules. . . . He had to pull the hay down with a pitchfork, spread it, put

the pitchfork down, then pick the pitchfork up. So he said, 'I drilled a hole in the handle of the pitchfork, and I took a wire and I ran it the full length of those stalls.' He said, 'When I had to spread the hay, the cable or the wire would keep the pitchfork in a good position and I didn't have to bend over to pick it up.' One day he was feeding the livestock, and he came to one particular mule. Just as he let go, the mule put his head down to eat the hay. L. B. Sharp let go of the fork. The fork went up in the air and came back down again right through the mule's ear. The mule, of course, didn't like that, so he kicked down the back of his stall and ran out. Mrs. Sharp [was] looking out of the kitchen window, and she [saw] this mule run into her flower and herb garden. . . . L. B. said, 'Well, that was the end of my second creative effort' (T. Rillo, personal communication, December 27, 2001).

[L. B. explained] 'One day I was riding the hay rake.' The hay rake had a metal seat and it had holes in it, and he went over a yellow jacket nest. He said, 'That evening, when I pulled my pants down to ask my mother to pull out those stingers, there was a yellow jacket stinger for every hole in that metal seat.' The bees had stung him from beneath. He said, 'That taught me a lot about if you have many hands doing the job, the job will get done.' He said, 'Delegation is personified in a hive of yellow jackets' (T. Rillo, personal communication, December 27, 2001).

Sharp later recounted the experience in a conference address. He summarized,

What you read in a book, you can easily forget, but what I got in the seat, I didn't forget very soon, and that is a part of realism we face in these things. You don't have to get stung that badly to have a lesson in outdoor education take root (Sharp, 1960a).

Emerging educational leader. An additional story from L. B.'s early years in Carbondale describes his first venture into education, into what would become the path to his future career into outdoor education.

> Before he went to college, he went to a one-room school-house, grades one to eight. When he was in the eighth grade, his teacher became ill. The school superintendent, who rode the circuit on a horse from rural school to rural school, asked [him] if he would teach the class. He was very much afraid . . . even though he was one of the oldest boys in the classroom. . . . L. B. Sharp began to teach the class reluctantly and with great fear that he would not succeed, but he did. He got so good at teaching, and he got so engrossed in interacting with these students that he said, 'I really thought an evil thing.' He said, 'I was hoping she'd never return for the rest of the year.' This was probably the spark, the catalyst, that gave him the idea that he'd like to go into education to be a teacher (T. Rillo, personal communication, December 27, 2001).

In Sharp's written account of this story years later, he told of his initial reluctance to teach the class. He admitted, "I didn't want to wish Miss Hartman any bad luck, but it would be all right with me if she wasn't able to come back next Friday noon" (Sharp, 1960a).

Sharp graduated from high school in Carbondale, where both of his parents had been continuously involved in the school system. Soon after graduating from high school, he served as the principal of a grammar school during the 1915–1916 school year in Quenemo, Kansas. The following year, he entered Kansas State Normal School in Emporia, Kansas (Sharp, 1930). He graduated in 1918 with a bachelor of science degree. His major field of study was in manual training, with minor studies in agriculture (Piercy, 1978). Kansas State was within an hour's drive of Carbondale. One of the narrators offered the following insight into L. B.'s college years and his continuous ties to the family farm.

> [L. B.] majored in physical education [also referred to as manual training], but never, never mentioned it publicly. He was a good athlete. He played football. He was also in track

and field. He ran and also threw the shot put and the discus. He used to call Emporia the 'college on the hill.' Well, it must have risen about six to eight inches above the rest of the terrain, but then it was a hill with Kansas being flat. . . . He went to Emporia, and in summer times he'd come back and work on the farm (T. Rillo, personal communication, December 27, 2001).

Navy, Marriage, and Michigan

During 1918, the same year of his college graduation, he married Alice Whitney, who was from Madison, Wisconsin, at the time (Piercy, 1978). Alice was born in Dane County, Wisconsin, on April 5, 1893 (Wisconsin Vital Records Index, 2002). Soon after marrying, during the final year of World War I, Sharp entered the U. S. Navy at the Great Lakes Naval Station, where he served as an ensign for a few years (Sharp, 1930).

Slightly later, from 1920 until 1923, Sharp was a "field organizer and representative" (Sharp, 1930, p. 115) in Michigan for the Playground and Recreation Association of America. Interestingly, in 1924, this association published an extensive 636-page book, *Camping Out: A Manual on Organized Camping*, in which Elbert K. Fretwell contributed a chapter on training camp leaders. At the time, Fretwell was a professor of education at Teachers College-Columbia University. Fretwell's chapter described the course in camp leadership he directed during the spring of 1923. It was referred to as the fourth such course taught at Teachers College (Playground and Recreation Association, 1924). Fretwell's course in 1923, or one taught soon after, was likely attended by Sharp, who had been a student of Fretwell's beginning in February of that year (Sharp, 1930). William Gould Vinal, then professor at Rhode Island College of Education, was listed as one of the leaders for this course (Playground and Recreation Association, 1924). Vinal, later to become one of Sharp's closest associates, worked with him for

several years at National Camp, established by Sharp in 1940 for outdoor leadership preparation.

Teachers College-Columbia University

In February of 1923, Sharp left the position in Michigan to begin graduate studies at Teachers College. He received his master's degree in physical education in 1924, and began work on his doctoral degree immediately afterward. His doctoral studies were completed in 1929 past the deadline for graduation in December of that year. His diploma was awarded in February of 1930 (Piercy, 1978). Sharp's dissertation, "Education and the Summer Camp: An Experiment," was one of the main events that led to the importance attributed to 1930 as a cornerstone year for outdoor education (Hammerman & Hammerman, 1980). In Sharp's dissertation, he acknowledged his gratitude to his committee members, J. F. Williams, E. K. Fretwell, D. H. Kulp, and F. G. Bosner (Sharp, 1930). His committee chair was Jesse Williams, "a highly regarded physical educator" (Wiener, 1965, p. 60).

While working on his doctoral studies, Sharp also served as a part-time faculty member in physical education at Columbia and at the nearby Horace Mann School. He assisted Fretwell with camp leadership courses from 1926 until Sharp left Columbia in 1929 (Sharp, 1930). According to Wiener (1965), Columbia University was "the first institution to begin educational work with the camping movement in 1920" (p. 61). As noted earlier, Sharp studied under John Dewey and William H. Kilpatrick during his years at Columbia (Rillo, 1980a, 1980b; Wiener, 1965).

Narrators shared their perspective on Sharp's years at Columbia University through the following descriptive statements:

> If I were to look at the basic influences [on Sharp's philosophy of outdoor education, they would be] the farm experience and then the experience at Columbia with these "New Educators" who were talking about small group learning [and] talking about experiential education long before that term was used. They were talking about getting learning back to the student. They, in turn, were influenced by Pestalozzi, by Froebel, by Comenius. The "New Educators" themselves were a vanguard of a new approach to emphasizing the community in education, using the community as a laboratory, going beyond the four walls of the classroom. When he was doing his doctorate there, he had the kind of influence that he transferred to camping education. You have to look at Columbia as being very important (T. Rillo, personal communication, December 27, 2001).

> He was there [at Columbia University] at the time when John Dewey and some of the pragmatic people were there. He was very well briefed on what those people were doing. John Dewey . . . went to several countries including Britain, the British Isles, and also to Russia and helped them to revamp their educational program, which included some outdoor education influences. . . . L. B. Sharp was at that university and knew him very well and talked with him and was probably

influenced by John Dewey a great deal and vice-versa" (E. Ambry, personal communication, February 10, 2002).

In response to whether Sharp kept in touch with Dewey, Kilpatrick, or Fretwell over the years, a narrator replied,

> Oh yes, very much so. I can remember him talking liberally with . . . those people (E. Ambry, personal communication, February 10, 2002).

During Sharp's final year or two at Columbia, an opportunity arose for him, due to his connections there. He was approached by key people involved with *Life* magazine's Fresh Air Farms and welfare agencies that served children from the New York area. It was an opportunity that, at the time unknown to Sharp, would launch his entire future career path of education in the outdoors.

— 2 —
The Middle Years (1925–1950);
Launching of a Career

Reorganization of Life's Fresh Air Farms

The Fresh Air Farms were founded in 1887 by John Ames Mitchell, and sponsored by *Life*'s Fresh Air Fund. The farms were established to provide a country summer vacation for children living in poverty in New York City. Children were identified as participants in the camps through local welfare agencies ("Life Camps," 1937). Sharp described Mitchell as both the owner and first president of the original *Life* magazine, founded in 1883. Mitchell, who lived in Ridgefield, Connecticut, was acquainted with a neighbor, Edwin Gilbert. Gilbert and Mitchell desired to provide "fresh air" services similar to those offered by the *New York Herald-Tribune* Fund that had been established in previous years. In the New York area, fresh air work of sending city children to stay at homes and farms in the country had been an endeavor established by the Children's Aid Society some time earlier (Yale Club, 1938).

Mitchell arranged to lease Gilbert's farm in 1891 in Branchville, Connecticut (Sharp, 1930), which was offered in later years at no charge to Life Publishing Company (Gilbert, 1898). The farm was used for both boys and girls, in conjunction with the continued use of private homes and farms until 1894, when the farm began to be used exclusively for *Life*'s Fresh Air work. In 1923, James Cox Brady offered the Brady estate for an additional Life Farm to be established. This farm was located near Pottersville, New Jersey, and became known as the Boys' Camp, or later, as Camp Raritan. That same year, the farm at Branchville, Connecticut, was renamed the Girls' Camp (Sharp, 1930).

During January of 1925, Sharp was approached by representatives of *Life*'s Fresh Air Fund and asked to visit the farms to make recommendations for their reorganization. This request resulted from suggestions by agents of the Charity Organization Society, who had visited the farms the previous year (Secretary of Life's Fresh Air Fund, 1925). At the time, Rev. and Mrs. U. O. Mohr were the managers of *Life*'s Fresh Air Farm at Branchville, and they lived in nearby Georgetown, Connecticut. Mohr and his wife, who had managed the farm for 25 years, were originally hired by John Mitchell (Mohr, 1925).

The circumstances surrounding the reorganization of Life's Fresh Air Farms were described through the following narrative segments:

> While [L. B.] was at Columbia, he was approached by the *Life* Fresh Air Farms. Edith Shatto King came . . . to the School of Education at Columbia to ask if there was someone there who could help them reorganize the Fresh Air Farms. . . . There were two newspapers [in New York], *Life* magazine and the *Herald-Tribune*. Each ran a Fresh Air Fund for poor kids in New York City, tenement kids. Mrs. King had received recommendations from some of the professors . . . including John Dewey, Boyd Bode, and William Heard Kilpatrick. All three recommended that she talk to L. B. Sharp. So she interviewed him, and he asked her, 'What do you do?' And she said, 'Well, we take the kids into the out-of-doors and to these camps.' . . . He said, 'What do you do at these camps?' And she said, 'Oh we give them an experience in the fresh air. We call them *Life*'s Fresh Air Farms.' So L. B. said to her,

'Well, I know you farm corn. And I know you farm beans. And I know you farm potatoes, but I've never heard anybody farming fresh air.' He said, 'That's a crop I haven't heard of before.' She didn't know quite what to make of this brash young man who was asking these questions (T. Rillo, personal communication, December 27, 2001).

He decided he would go and take a look. He went first to the girls' camp in Branchville, Connecticut. Here were these girls, the counselors were eating from one menu and the campers were eating from another menu. L. B. Sharp said that if you looked at the quality and the taste of the food, you would want to eat what the counselors were eating. He said they were all jammed up [with] maybe 30 to 40 girls in a unit with two counselors. It was militarily set up so that the two counselors could watch the cabins arranged in co-linear array. . . . The same thing was true down at Camp Raritan with the boys (T. Rillo, personal communication, December 27, 2001).

L. B. Sharp said, 'If I'm going to take this reorganization, I want to be able to have a free rein.' . . . You let me make some changes and allow me the freedom to do so,' he said, '[and] I will take on the study.' . . . He was given the job of director of Life Camps. He changed the name from 'farms' to 'camps,' going back to the same story about farming air or farming kids. So, it became Life Camps instead of Life Fresh Air Farms (T. Rillo, personal communication, December 27, 2001).

On January 28, 1925, a brief, two-paragraph letter was written to the Mohr's announcing that a meeting of the directors of *Life*'s Fresh Air Fund had been held that day and that the positions previously held by the Mohrs would be terminated as of April 1 of that year (Secretary of Life's Fresh Air Fund, 1925). An accompanying page stated that a decision had been made to hire Sharp as the new director of both of the Fresh Air Farms because he "has had professional training in this line of work" (Secretary of Life's Fresh Air Fund, 1925, p. 2).

Tom Rillo described Sharp's first attempts at hiring new staff members with the following explanation:

> When [L. B.] was given the job of executive director. . . . he started with Girls' Camp first. . . . He wanted responsible counselors, counselors who could work well under this plan. The first counselor that he hired was a lady by the name of Rya Gelavitz. He went to this Girl Scout camp, and he said, 'I heard about a good counselor here. Her name is Rya Gelavitz. Can you tell me where I might find her?' . . . This woman director said, 'She went . . . up that hill into the woods two weeks ago. We haven't seen her since.' L. B. Sharp turned around and rubbed his hands together and smiled and said, 'That's the counselor for me.' And so, Rya became the first counselor that he employed for Life Camps. And Rya stayed with him right to the end. She was a teacher in Massachusetts. He began to put a staff together, dedicated people with skills. How he managed to get these people together! Sure, they bickered. Sure, they had their jealousies . . . but when it came to the program itself, these people jelled like a finely tuned engine (T. Rillo, personal communication, December 27, 2001).

One of the first reorganization efforts Sharp made was after the summer 1925 camp sessions. To the organizations that sent children to the camps that summer he mailed a brief report mentioning an average weight gain of the children of two and three-quarters pounds. He also included a survey with 17 open-ended questions that would be used in the reorganization efforts. The survey stated, "We are anxious to raise the standard of our camps as high as possible in line with the most progressive and constructive tendencies in education and social service" (Sharp, 1925, p. 3). The survey listed his title as director of *Life*'s Summer Camps, using the name *camps* rather than the previously used *farms*.

Sharp also began his plan to change the camps from a charity organization with a centralized, regimented approach to decentralized camps built around the concept of holistic child development.

A statement of aims for the Life Camps was soon developed. It maintained that the aim of the camp program was

> to provide desirable camp situations in which the camper may participate, under skilled leadership, for the greatest improvement in their health, happiness, and citizenship. We are especially interested in the development of the leadership ability of the campers (Sharp, 1930, p. 38–39)

Ed Ambry offered this description of what Sharp was aspiring to accomplish for children through the Life Camp program:

> The principle of his whole program was that he believed that children should come to camp, and the basic program was just one, two, three. . . . They had to have food, shelter, and some kind of spiritual uplift. . . . It was like a family for a whole month living together. There were ten children and two counselors. Nobody had ever heard of that kind of a staff, camping under canvas. In these camps, the program was camping. Living in the out-of-doors. There were no baseballs. They didn't do anything that you could do in the city (E. Ambry, personal communication, February 10, 2002).

As he was completing his doctoral dissertation at Columbia University, a fulltime position became available for Sharp in Chicago. This position would allow Sharp to continue his work with Life Camps, returning to New York and New Jersey during the summer months.

Lab School, University of Chicago

In the fall of 1929, Sharp took a position at the University Lab School at the University of Chicago. His position there was as the head of the Physical Education and Health Department for elementary and high school students (Fine, 1987). That November, the new Sunny Gymnasium for the high school students at the Lab School was dedicated ("Physical education staff meeting," 1932).

Three years later, in a memorandum from a meeting of the physical education staff members, what appears to be a speech made by Sharp indicated that high school curriculum changes and budget cuts had resulted in his job termination as of the end of the school year ("Physical education staff meeting," 1932). From 1929 until he left Chicago, Sharp had continued to serve as the part-time director of *Life*'s Summer Camps. He remained at the University of Chicago until the spring of 1933. At that time, Sharp and his family returned to New York where he continued his work with the Fresh Air Fund camps (Piercy, 1978).

Executive Director of *Life*'s Fresh Air Camps

Sharp continued to implement educational goals into the curricula and programs of Life Camps. In November of 1935, Sharp was arranging a camp leadership course, in conjunction with C. L. Brownell of Columbia University, to be held at the Life Camps. Sharp felt that the interest shown by Columbia indicated the recognition his work at the camps had received (Sharp, 1935).

Soon after, in 1936, Time, Inc. purchased *Life* magazine (Outdoor Education Association, n.d.). At that time, the Fresh Air Fund changed its name to Life Camps, Incorporated and gave Sharp a full-time position and the title of executive director of Life Camps (Piercy, 1978). An article in the *Time* weekly magazine stated that the camps had just become the "responsibility of *Life the Picture Weekly*, published by Time, Inc." ("Life Camps," 1937, p. 28). At that time, the camps enrolled only children who were referred by the New York City Family Welfare Agencies. The operational costs of the camps were to be paid by *Time* readers whereby "every dollar sent in by contributors would be converted into one full day in the country for one boy or girl" (p. 28). Ed Ambry explained,

> If you looked on the back of an old *Time* magazine . . . there was a big dollar sign there that said, 'A dollar a day keeps a camper at camp.' When a magazine sold, a dollar of every one of those magazines [was collected], millions of them. It was a big money maker (E. Ambry, personal communication, February 10, 2002).

By July 12, 1937, there were three Life Camps. The Girls' Camp was still in Branchville, Connecticut, and was being directed by Lois Goodrich. Camp Raritan for boys ages eight to sixteen was still in Pottersville, New Jersey, and was directed by William L. Gunn. An additional camp for boys ages thirteen to sixteen had been established on a private 750-acre tract of land in the Pocono Mountains near Matamoras, Pennsylvania. This was Camp Pole Bridge, and it was directed by Martin J. Feely ("Life Camps," 1937).

The following narrated segments by Tom Rillo provide a partial description of the Life Camps:

> [L. B. became] very familiar with Bill Palmer. Bill Palmer was, what you would call today, the CEO, the executive of Life and Time Incorporated. He had a home in Matamoras, Pennsylvania. It was called Pole Bridge. That was where one of the Life Camps was located . . . and so L. B. got his support very early on in his camping education approach and especially with Life Camps. . . . [Palmer] looked at this thing [and] said, 'Hey, there's some great things happening to these kids. They're living together. They're solving their own problems. They're planning their own menus. They're going down to the camp store and buying their own food.' They planned their own aims and objectives for every activity. Sanitation, food, health, woodcraft—all these things had aims and objectives. They sat down with their counselors and wrote them down at the beginning of every camp. This was the decentralized plan. He saw how remarkable this was in causing changes. These kids came from the Lower East Side, from Harlem, from Hell's Kitchen. Girls and boys came from impoverished tenements of New York City just boil[ing] over with the heat of the summer and crowded conditions. Children of immigrants and black kids [came] too. It was just wonderful to see how they all came and lived together. This was long before the racial equality movement started and all that. It was there in a total living situation of the small group camp. I remember how we got along. There was no hatred or anything like that. . . . It was funded. They were all on camp

scholarships (T. Rillo, personal communication, December 27, 2001).

[As a child], I was given a scholarship from a civic group in Summit, [New Jersey] to attend a camp, and that camp was Camp Raritan in Pottersville, New Jersey. I met L. B. Sharp then, for the first time. It was 1938. I didn't know anything about him, or who he was, or what he was, except that he was the director, the executive director. He was over Bill Gunn. Bill Gunn was the director of Camp Raritan. We lived under the decentralized plan of camping. I lived in the covered wagon village unit. I went there for two summers. The second summer I lived in hogans or covered sleds. . . . That was the Life Camp that was located at Lake Mashipacong located in northern New Jersey. It was situated in High Point State Park adjacent to Stokes State Forest (T. Rillo, personal communication, December 27, 2001).

Building of a new girls' camp. By October of 1938, the camps together were serving about 250 children, all of whom attended the camps for a month during the summer at no charge. The camps continued to be funded by contributions of Time, Inc. and the readers of *Time*'s publications. Sharp was in the process of building a fourth camp on a 1,000-acre piece of forested land on Lake Mashipacong in the Kittatinny Mountains in northern New Jersey near Sussex. The plan was to build a new camp for girls and a center for training outdoor leaders, a center for what was later to become National Camp ("New frontier," 1938). The new Girls' Camp was completed, and the location was moved from Connecticut to New Jersey in 1939 ("Life Camp history pertinent to Camp Raritan," n.d.). The camp adjoined over 25,000 acres of state parks and forests. The facility was also within hiking distance from the Appalachian Trail and from High Point State Park (Partridge, 1943). The state park was the location of the highest elevation point in the state of New Jersey. The following narratives discuss the plans to build the new camps.

[L. B. Sharp] was looking for a site to come down out of Connecticut and to bring Girls' Camp closer and also to start National Camp. He went to the tobacco heiress, Doris Duke, in Somerville, New Jersey. Somerville was very close to [Camp] Raritan at Pottersville. . . . He'd been traipsing around up there in High Point State Park, and he found this parcel of land that was owned privately. It wasn't owned by the state. . . . He asked the caretaker up there who owned the property. . . . He met with Doris Duke [the owner, who] listened to his proposal. . . . She leased her property to Life and Time, Incorporated, and that's how that piece of property got started (T. Rillo, personal communication, December 27, 2001).

I met L. B. Sharp in 1938, which was 64 years ago. . . . I was working for a company that . . . imported and exported a lot of building materials. . . . I noticed a big shipment was being made. It was [for] building a new camp in Sussex County, New Jersey. When I was getting near the end of that work year, I took the address and telephone numbers and I called L. B. in New York City. He invited me to come into New York City and have an interview with him to be a counselor at the camp. From then on, I knew him intimately (E. Ambry, personal communication, February 10, 2002).

Sharp had engaged in a tradition of sending out a card each year around Christmas on behalf of Life Camps. The cards usually displayed a photograph taken at one of the camps and often a poem written by Sharp himself. The card for 1938, which displayed a photo of a creek meandering through the snow-covered forest at the new camp location under construction at Lake Mashipacong, included the following poem by Sharp:

Nature
Peace-quiet-grandeur,
Majesty-beauty-rhythm,
Any part of it, all of it,
Anytime, all the time, night and day,
Yuletide, springtime, summer, autumn-

Everchanging, growing, creating,
Never still-silent and smooth,
Though forceful-
Softens, inspires one's soul
Giving new visions, new hopes-
Raises one's spiritual self.
Strength.
So full of reverence and companionship,
We need what she holds.
Blanketed in snow, drenched in rain-
Crowned with green, tinted with gold-
Her hidden mysteries beckon-
Come! And linger. (Sharp, 1938)

One of the most unique aspects of the program at Life Camps was what Sharp called "decentralized camping." Decentralized camping entailed small groups of about seven campers and two counselors living together in one unit of the camp facilities. These small family-style units were responsible for providing their own shelter, cooking their own food, and planning their daily activities (Partridge, 1943). Activities that could be done in the city, such as organized sports, were avoided. Rather, hiking, exploring, and outdoor skills were advocated (Partridge, 1943). The sleeping and living structures at the camps were hand-constructed by the campers and counselors. Some examples included tepees, lean-tos, round-tos, and large sleds or hogans, which were long canvas-covered Native American structures with roofs supported by curved saplings (*Adventures in camping*, 1943).

The camps promoted frontier and Native American themes. The center of each camp was known as the Village, which normally had a dining hall where campers routinely ate one meal a day, an administration building, and a library. Sometimes there also might be a trading post, cobbler's shop, and blacksmith shop, similar to those found in pioneer villages (Partridge, 1943). Overnight trips away from the campsites were common for the older campers, who often used horse-drawn covered wagons.

The idea of decentralized camping was developed over several years before the third Life Camp, Pole Bridge, was constructed near Matamoras, Pennsylvania. Until 1934, the program at the Boys' Camps and the Girls' Camp were centralized and departmentalized, with the exception of the Outpost Camps developed at each site in 1928. Between 1928 and 1934, the Outpost Camps experimented with overnight camping, hiking trips, outdoor cooking, and other activities conducted outdoors away from the main camp areas. In 1934, a five-year process was begun to convert the remainder of the camp programs over to a small group, outpost-type of operation ("Life Camp history pertinent to Camp Raritan," n.d.).

Narrators offered their recollections of the decentralized camping model promoted by Sharp throughout the camps:

> Where did he get the concept of the shelters? Shacks and Shanties by Dan Beard. Also the influence of the Native American and the tepees and the covered wagons [were] because of his family's experience in coming from New Jersey. . . . He put the hogans on a sled so you could move them around. No unit was ever static, so you could move them around as you wore out the land or impacted it. . . . He was very ahead of his time in terms of use of land and the ecology of location (T. Rillo, personal communication, December 27, 2001).

> We put in our menu and they would provide it for us. We were given the first year, the one I remember vividly, was $.50 a day per person, so $5.00 a day to feed all ten of us. We could get whatever we wanted. We had to submit our menu to the dietician to make sure it was nutritious and balanced. We explained to the boys, all of whom said 'We'd love to have steak.' If you love to have steak, you can do it, but you have to get the cheapest of everything all month long almost to do it. In the process of working out the menu, getting a good dessert or steak or something special that they all liked, they had to plan the menu with inexpensive foods. Those kids

that didn't know arithmetic before they started, they knew arithmetic by the time we got done, because they had to do the calculations. The counselors did not (L. Huntley, personal communication, March 15, 2002).

We ended up with good menus and our rare treat days. . . . We would put the menu in meeting the cost, and then the dietician approved it. If the dietician was not satisfied, she came back and told us to make some modifications, which again, we did with the boys. Another illustration of learning arithmetic (L. Huntley, personal communication, March 15, 2002).

He really invented what was called the 'small camp concept.' We lived out in the woods with the children. We had tepees or we had other kinds of structures, most of which the young people would build for themselves. You went to the dining room for just one meal a day. The other times, you stayed in your small camp and lived together like a family. . . . That kind of philosophy really changed camping forever (E. Ambry, personal communication, February 10, 2002).

L. B. brought a lot of people into decentralized camping. A major reason is because it had less impact on the environment. It was quieter. The spirituality was felt better. You were conscious of what you were doing with the environment [such as with] building fires. We talked about the forest in the process of building fires. Some woods are good for starting fires. Some are for building coals. Some are good for different kinds of carving. You gained an appreciation for the outdoors and the role that each of these things have in the big world. . . . We studied and watched the little critters and the things that make up the outdoors, the flora, the fauna, the geology, the hydrology of the area. When you're living it, in these small groups, you have a greater understanding and appreciation because you are living and working with it every day (R. Christie, personal communication, May 9, 2002).

In utilizing the outdoors and broadening the base of experiences and the problem-solving approaches, the interaction approaches to learning were a very strong part of what [L. B.] was doing. It was not just getting people out, but it was the learning strategies that were involved and the interaction between the leader or the teacher and the kids in a very humane way so that people had the freedom to try things and to experiment. They had this big field to roam around in with their minds. That probably would be the most significant aspect of what he was doing. While the environment was important, it was the medium that he worked in, and he was working in the mind. He had this great feeling for the outdoors and for cultures and for history. An appreciation for people who lived close to the land (R. Christie, personal communication, May 9, 2002).

In Sharp's dissertation study, an analysis of the Life Camp reorganization process, one of his recommendations was the expansion of regular camp sessions from one or two weeks to a longer period of time so that campers could have the opportunity for increased cognitive, emotional, and social growth. By the completion of his study in 1930, he had begun to expand the length of his programs (Sharp, 1930) until by 1938, only month-long sessions were offered ("Life Camp history pertinent to Camp Raritan," n.d.). Ed Ambry recollected,

> Most of the kinds of camps that young people in New York City, especially those who did not have a lot of money, were sent there for one week. . . . His idea was that that didn't do much good. . . . He organized his camps so that the children would come for four weeks. . . . He based that whole philosophy on the fact that these young people would be changed, or that there was time to work with them, time to understand them, time to understand the education (E. Ambry, personal communication, February 10, 2002).

> Some of the times, when the children came to his camps, and they had to go home . . . several of the kids ran away, and then the buses couldn't find them. Then, after the buses left, they were still in camp, which was great (E. Ambry, personal communication, February 10, 2002).

First experiment in school camping. In 1937 Johanna M. Lindlof was the chair of the Committee on Instructional Affairs of the Board of Education for the City of New York. During September of that year, she began the first of a series of proposals for the New York Public Schools to fund a school camping program for "underprivileged children" (*Adventures in camping*, 1943, p. 9). The Board of Education voted down the proposals. Lindlof finally secured private funding for the program by establishing the Johanna M. Lindlof Camp Fund for Public School Children. Lindlof and several New York City school principals designed the objectives and curricular aims for the program based on the "democratic educational and social philosophy as outlined by the Educational Policies Commission of the National Education Association" (p. 10). This committee determined that the program at Life Camps was closely aligned with these statements, and arranged for a group of 110 New York City school children to attend the three Life Camps in the summer of 1939. The funds raised by the Lindlof Camp Fund were depleted after that first summer. Fiorello H. LaGuardia, then mayor of New York City, led a campaign to continue the project. Mrs. Franklin Delano Roosevelt was a member of the fund-raising campaign.

Earlier that year, Lindlof had received a letter from the principal of Public School 3 stating intentions to "launch a campaign for the colored schools in Brooklyn, the purpose of which will be to contribute to the Lindlof Camp Fund so that in 1940 colored pupils will be sent to camp under your auspices" (Gillis, 1939, p. 1). Soon afterward, a similar letter to Sharp from the Harlem Branch of the Young Men's Christian Association, the West Harlem Council of Social Agencies, and the New York Chapter of the State Conference on Negro Welfare voiced concern that "no Negro boys will be included among the campers" (Craft, 1939, p. 1) at Life Camps. A conference was requested by representatives of those agencies, yet decisions regarding enrolling African-American students in the camps had still not been made as of December 1939 (Lindlof, 1939). Finally, by the summer of 1940, arrangements were made for 25 "Negro children" (*Adventures in camping*, 1943, p. 11) to attend the camps.

The activities of the Lindlof Camp Committee were operated as a series of experiments from 1939 until 1943. Physical and social progress records were kept on each funded camper. These records were added to throughout the following school year by a social worker employed by the committee and were subsequently turned over to the schools where the children were enrolled (*Adventures in camping*, 1943, p. 12). *Adventures in Camping* provided a comprehensive report giving a description of the camps, the program, the camper progress records, and recommendations to the Board of Education of New York City. The first recommendation was for an experiment to be conducted in 1944 in which classes of fourth or fifth grade New York school children would attend camp for a month of the school year with their teachers for the purpose of determining if the New York City school system could improve its school curricula through camping.

The New York Experiment. Finally, in 1947, Sharp was hired by the Board of Education of New York City to conduct a comprehensive study of educational outcomes derived from an outdoor education experience (*Extending education through camping*, 1948). This "significant pioneer experiment in school camping and outdoor education" (Rillo, 1980a, p. 26) is often referred to as the New York City Experiment or the School Camp Experiment. The methodology, outcomes, and conclusions derived from the study were discussed in detail in a hardbound book entitled *Extending Education through Camping*, published in 1948.

Sharp arranged for 62 fifth and seventh grade students to attend Life Camps for three weeks. A control group was arranged at two schools in New York City. The experimental group at the camps built their own shelters, purchased food, prepared their own meals, and determined their daily activities. All of the participants were tested before and after the experiment in nature study, science and health, vocabulary, arithmetic, and an interest inventory (*Extending education through camping*, 1948).

The results from the New York study revealed that the mean scores were higher for the experimental group in eight out of ten post-tests. Of these eight tests, five were found to be statistically significant. The gains for the fifth grade experimental group were greater than for the seventh grade group in the subjects of arithmetic, vocabulary, nature study, and the interest inventory. The largest gains for the seventh grade experimental group were in the interest inventory. The control group for the experiment had no gains that were statistically significant. The summary of conclusions stated, "The test results indicate initial and final superiority of the experimental group, with many of the differences in their favor being statistically significant" (*Extending education through camping*, 1948, p. 62). The New York Experiment is called one of Sharp's greatest contributions, "for it established the fact that outdoor education was academically sound and could be an extension of the regular curricular program" (Rillo, 1980a, p. 26). Narrators offered the following comments about the New York Experiment:

> There were weaknesses of the '47 experiment: three weeks as opposed to five days, camping education instead of correlated activities to the curriculum. The psychological testing was not over a longer period of time. It was too short. We do it so much differently today than we did then, but at that time, it was right (T. Rillo, personal communication, December 27, 2001).

The studies that he did in New York City on the outdoor program, the three-week studies, those were the most comprehensive outdoor education studies that have ever been completed on school camping. These were the basis for the school camping program, except that his was a three to four week program and most school camping programs were only for one week. At that time, the teachers weren't doing a lot of school site studies (R. Christie, personal communication, May 9, 2002).

Establishment of National Camp

The accomplishments at Life Camps were beginning to draw national attention and many visitors. The March of Time filmed a documentary of the camps entitled, "Youth in Camps" (March of Time, 1937). There was soon a growing demand for trained leaders in the new camping education techniques being used at Life Camps (Partridge, 1943). In June of 1940, this growing demand led to the opening of National Camp. Located on the same property as the Girls' Camp, National Camp was a facility specifically for the training of outdoor teachers and leaders.

During the first year of National Camp, six-week summer institutes were offered in camp leadership. These courses would later be referred to as *outdoor teacher education institutes*. Through New York University, students could earn six hours of graduate credit for participating in the institutes. The following summer, two-week sessions were offered for students earning teaching certificates through any of the six New Jersey State Teachers Colleges (Rillo, 1980a).

Interviewees described some of the features of National Camp with the following comments:

> National Camp was very prominent. . . . It was the same location as the Girls' Camp, but it was in a different part. It was like an institute, like a college campus, but all concentrated on outdoor education. . . . There were a number of professors who would come and work with him and sort of 'frame out' a faculty for it. . . . Mostly, it operated in the summer, but during the wintertime, they also had conferences (E. Ambry, personal communication, February 10, 2002).

> [L. B.'s] leadership significantly influenced schools, colleges, universities, agencies, and professional organizations. . . . Responsibilities were developed through participation contributing to the success of the group. Direct learning experiences were encouraged to teach effectively in the out-of-doors . . .

Self-reliance opportunities needed to be made available to live comfortably and happily in the out-of-doors (E. Morrison, personal communication, May 11, 2002).

He set up National Camp because it needed to be done. . . . At one point, every major outdoor education leader in the country had come through L. B.'s National Camp. Every one of them (R. Christie, personal communication, May 9, 2002).

My first meeting with Dr. L. B. Sharp occurred during the summer in 1948 when I enrolled as a student in the outdoor education program conducted at National Camp, Sussex, New Jersey, at Lake Mashipacong. . . . The program cooperated with the School of Education of New York University providing graduate credit for completion of a 'problem' study. National Camp was funded by Life Camps, Incorporated in response to a felt need for advanced leadership in the field in the outdoor and camping education. I was interested in pursuing this field professionally (E. Morrison, personal communication, May 11, 2002).

We went to Springfield College and during [my] freshman year, L. B. Sharp was a lecturer at the college on Outdoor Education and National Camp. . . . We were invited, a group of ten students and a college professor, to come to National Camp. We went as a group. I was quite surprised at the technique and even the layout of the camp. National Camp was built on tepees, 'round-tos,' covered wagons, hogans, that type of small camp [shelter] (C. Emanuelson, personal communication, January 21, 2002).

National Camp was founded on two principles. One was that American youth should live and learn with competent leaders who can help them succeed in the daily tasks of outdoor living. The other principle was that the only way such an endeavor was possible was for educators at all levels to experience such a program and then carry out similar camping programs in their own communities (Partridge, 1943). Therefore, each student who attended National

Camp worked on a research paper, referred to as a "National Camp Problem," wherein plans were made to apply outdoor teaching to the students' home communities.

One of the narrators, Ellie Morrison, who had been a student at National Camp, described her research problem below:

> My National Camp 'study problem,' as our paper was identified for graduate credit through New York University, focused on the college curriculum where I was teaching [at the College of St. Joseph in Cincinnati, Ohio] in 1948–49. The title of my paper was, 'Motivating the Students of a Small Women's College to an Enjoyment and Appreciation of the World of the Out-of-Doors.' This project motivated me to extend learning in the out-of-doors and educating with various departments and the community on this college site (E. Morrison, personal communication, May 11, 2002).

Leadership preparation through practice. Teachers applied the philosophy of learning through direct educative experiences at all of the children's camps and for adult learners at the National Camp. Although National Camp sessions included informational sessions about teaching, hygiene, discipline, and other leadership issues, these students also participated in all of the physical lessons and activities carried out in the Life Camp programs with children. Some of the National Camp activities are discussed in the narratives below:

> Activities at National Camp focused on studies in natural history. Students learned through field trips, conferences, and research projects. Subjects included tree studies with Moosewood Harlow, orienteering with Phil Walker, nature crafts with Rya [Gelavitz], music and dancing with E. DeAlton Partridge, stump scouting with Captain Bill Vinal, and adventure trips and wildlife with Reynold Carlson. Other fields of experiences shared with staff included fire building, shelters, water studies, map and compass, food services, drama, creative writing, journaling, geology, farm life, night

sky, birding, and studies in natural history (E. Morrison, personal communication, May 11, 2002).

I was inspired to express some of these experiences in a poem captured in my camp notebook. . . . I think it summarizes the relationship of particular subjects [studied at National Camp]. The date is July 27, 1948.

Humanities created in the woods a sitting
I sit me down upon this log
and to the wind my cares will toss.
For in the woods I'm ever free.
My thoughts race on most joyfully.
I gaze at tree, at fern, at flower
At rest out here in Mother Nature's bower.
The smells are sweet. The sounds are soft.
As blue sky peeks through the branch aloft.
The leaves throw a shadow round
A small life crawling on the ground.
With water lapping over the rocks
Time has no end. We need no clocks.
I often wish each man might know
Just how the wild things live and grow.
Live trees are tall or bent to earth
These are the crafts of greatest worth.
(E. Morrison, personal communication, May 11, 2002)

During that time [at National Camp], we had several sessions where we would have a campfire and [L. B.] would say, 'Okay, who wants to start the fire?' Somebody would volunteer. Well, he would give you a choice, either flint and steel or fire-by-friction [bow and drill]. A couple of us tried it. Fortunately, I had been in Boys Scouts before the war, so I was very familiar with fire by friction, so I lit our first fire there (C. Emanuelson, personal communication, January 21, 2002).

We had to cook our own meals for part of the time. We had planned chicken. We got down to the dining room, or where they had supplies and so forth. [L. B.] was standing there and we were picking up all of our things. One of the guys said, 'Well, where are the chickens?' He picked up a gunny sack. 'Here they are.' They were alive. . . . With L. B. Sharp and the staff at National Camp, it was all that kind of activity where you were put to the test at every opportunity. . . . Whenever he could, he would challenge you and work you into a situation where you had to come through. [For example, on] the covered wagon trips that we took, you're responsible for what you need. You planned your menus and worked out the program. I don't ever remember him saying that you shouldn't do this or that. Just work it out and try to do it (C. Emanuelson, personal communication, January 21, 2002).

Basically, most everything was a story with [L. B.]. Take the fire-by-friction. Once we got the fire going that day, and got it started, he [would ask], 'What do you think is the best tree? What is the best wood to develop this kind of an instrument?' Take a Number 10 can that you would make coffee [in]? . . . Well, a Number 10 tin can has quite a story, too, because it has to be just so. The holes have to be in balance on both sides of the can. You have to get a strong enough wire to . . . turn it and it takes 'years and years and years' of experience. You have to have the right amount of water in the can and you put the right amount of influence into what you've got in there and it takes 'years and years and years' of experience. . . . He would wind this into a story that would take a half an hour. And the same thing with fire-by-friction (C. Emanuelson, personal communication, January 21, 2002).

Working with children through National Camp. The students who attended National Camp experienced intensive leadership preparation in all phases of camping and education in the out-of-doors. If the National Camp sessions were held when the children were in attendance at the Life Camps, the students would apply their learning through working with the children. Some of the narrators' recollections of working with the children are recounted in the following paragraphs:

At National Camp . . . the kids planned their meals, their menus, their program. We were working with decentralized camping. . . . We worked through the daily living routines. We worked through our daily program routines. We set up our codes of behavior. It was group-oriented and worked out within the group (R. Christie, personal communication, May 9, 2002).

When we were at National Camp . . . we had kids that were five, six, seven years old. . . . [We] took the kids out to Shohola Wilderness . . . and set up camp. . . . One of the philosophies we had, when we went out to this area, we were driving our campers to and camping within a few hundred yards of the same site we were using every summer—One of the things you had to look for was to see if you could find evidence of where any of the other groups had stayed while they were there. So we had six year olds and seven year olds. They were out poking around seeing what they could find. . . . In trying to make it so that nobody can tell that you've been camped in the area, we were doing this at National Camp back in the '50s with L. B. at the same time or before Paul [Petzoldt] and other people were doing that in the back country. Paul was considered the pioneer in minimal impact camping tech-niques . . . but L. B. was 10, 20 years ahead of that. So we were very conscious of the environment and keeping it a natural environment (R. Christie, personal communication, May 9, 2002).

Leadership institutes for the New Jersey State Colleges. The idea for the New Jersey State College institutes in outdoor leader-ship preparation was launched by Robert H. Morrison, the state di-rector of Teacher Training in the New Jersey State Department of Education in the early 1940s. The first of these institutes was held at National Camp from June 17 through June 27, 1942, and was attended by 32 students from the six state colleges (Life Camps, Inc., 1942). The New Jersey institutes provided two hours of col-lege credit to the students (Partridge, 1943). In a memo outlining this first institute for the New Jersey State Colleges, Sharp wrote,

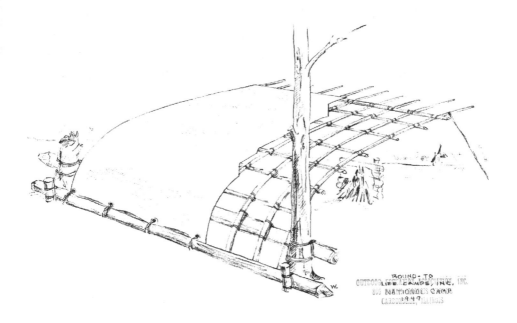

"This Camping Education Institute is considered a beginning of the movement in New Jersey. It should grow and expand in many directions" (Life Camps, Inc., 1942, p. 5). In the program for this first institute, Sharp was listed as "Director of National Camp, Executive Director of Life Camps, Inc., Special Lecturer New York University" (p. 4).

In December of 1943, E. K. Fretwell, a professor in physical education and one of Sharp's doctoral committee members from Teachers College – Columbia University, wrote a letter to Sharp regarding the first New Jersey Camping Education Institute. Fretwell stated, "Here is actually something new both in subject matter and method in education. My heartiest congratulations in your vision and what you have already achieved!" (Fretwell, 1943, p. 1). In 1942, the New York State Teachers Colleges also joined National Camp in holding two-week sessions for college credit (Rillo, 1980a).

Coining the term. That same year, Sharp wrote to Dave Brumbaugh alerting him of an article he had just submitted to the *Educational*

Forum (Sharp, 1943b). This article, "Outside the Classroom," appeared in the May 1943 issue of *Educational Forum* (Sharp, 1943a), and was probably the first printed appearance of the term *outdoor education* (Knapp, 2000). Tom Rillo described his recollections of the term's formation as,

> L. B. Sharp said, 'You know, we have to do something about this term. It has its limitations, 'camping education.' You have to go to camp. He said, 'There's nothing that can be done back at the school if you call it 'camping.' You can't do 'camping education' stepping outside the classroom and using the school grounds or a nearby park.' He said, 'We need to adopt a terminology that would be inclusive of those experiences that we can have back in the community and back in the school grounds.' And so he coined the term 'outdoor education' (T. Rillo, personal communication, December 27, 2001).

Vesper services. A tradition that was an integral part of the Life Camps and National Camp program were Sunday vesper services. The criteria for designing the vespers identified by William Vinal were that the services should a) be concerned with the immediate camp environment, b) focus on topics broader than the everyday affairs of the camp, c) teach a great message or ethical story, d) be nondenominational, e) use simple, understandable language, and f) be filled with singing and poetry readings (Vinal, 1944). Explanations of the vesper services are provided in the following narratives:

> Whenever we were in camp on Sunday, we always had our vesper services. Singing was a big part of National Camp. . . . There would always be a vesper service on Sunday. [L. B. would] take part, too. . . . They'd be in an area where there's a brook or at Pole Bridge. They'd be out in the open on a high point area where there's a terrific vista. That wasn't too far from [L. B.'s] tepee. He always lived in a tepee at camp (C. Emanuelson, personal communication, January 21, 2002).

We had vesper services at every camp and every program whether it was [for] adults or children. They were given responsibilities for vesper services. There would be readings from scripture at these vesper services. . . . [L. B.] would sometimes speak at these vespers or others, but always a camper [was] in charge, always a camper. They were responsible for planning vespers. . . . Usually, he had a fire no matter what time the vespers were, usually in the evening with a fire burning (T. Rillo, personal communication, December 27, 2001).

[L. B.] always held what he called a 'vespers' service. . . . He influenced the School of Conservation children's camp where I worked. . . . That program was influenced by L. B. Sharp because of Tom Rillo and the director named Cliff Emanuelson and his wife Ginger. They went through National Camp as students. So, my experience in camping as a counselor really followed a version of L. B. Sharp's philosophy. Vespers were ecumenical, nature-based services based on what L. B. Sharp had taught those leaders. That's an example of how L. B. Sharp still lives today through the people he influenced. If they are not around, their students still carry parts of L. B.'s philosophy. It's amazing that his power still exists today (C. Knapp, personal communication, December 19, 2001).

I never did go to a vesper service at the Pole Bridge Camp, but I did as a counselor participate in the L. B. Sharp-type of vespers at the School of Conservation. It was [at] a summer camp called Camp Wapalanne. . . . [L. B.] would very clearly write and speak about spiritual development as one of the objectives of his programs. His work started in camping and then was carried over into the outdoor education in the schools. Later, carrying the spiritual activities into schools became a sticky issue and so the objective of spiritual development fell by the wayside (C. Knapp, personal communication, December 19, 2001).

He was in the Protestant faith, but I think he was pretty much interdenominational. We had vesper services every Sunday.

We were looking and talking about the world around us in that aspect. . . . We had Jewish and Christian kids. We had a broad variety of kids there and there was very definite spirituality (R. Christie, personal communication, May 9, 2002).

[L. B.] wasn't a church going individual. He interacted with enough people around him who were, but then he used to say that he went to church in the cathedral of the out-of-doors and that he got close to God. At that time, I didn't know enough about spirituality to know that, well, you have church because of the community aspect of it. 'But I have my community,' he would say today. . . . He didn't see any need for an organized church. In fact, he said one time, he said, 'You know, Christ did not have a church but a number of faith communities everywhere.' He said, 'A church is built as a shelter for people to come together but without the church, it would still be church' (T. Rillo, personal communication, December 27, 2001).

Changes in funding, changes due to war. In the fall of 1944, there were changes proposed by Time, Inc. pertaining to its relationship with and corporate funding of the three Life Camps and National Camp. In 1944, Time provided annual funding for the camps in the amount of $30,000, which was one-fifth of Time's total charity budget. In a September 1944 memo crafted by executives from Time, a statement was made that "neither Life Camps or National Camp represent a logical corporate charity for Time, Inc." (Time, Inc., 1944, p. 1).

The reason given for proposed removal of future funding was that "there is no corporate justification for spending so large a percentage of total contributions to charity on a venture that is in essence so far removed from Time, Inc.'s principal interests and activities" (Time, Inc., 1944, p. 1). A further harsh statement in the memo stated, "The camps neither contribute to the corporate public relations of Time, Inc. nor to the private education and enlightenment of its editors" (p. 1). The memo also stated that Time expected Life Camps and National Camp to begin the process of finding alternative sources of funding and to eventually become self-supporting. It was also suggested that the camps might benefit by being absorbed by a larger national organization catering to underprivileged children and that one day the need for National Camp might cease to exist (p. 2).

During the World War II years of 1943, 1944, and 1945, Pole Bridge Camp was closed due to staff shortages, as were many summer camps during that period. The director at Pole Bridge, Martin Feely, served as interim-director for William Gunn, the director at Camp Raritan, who had been called into military service ("Life Camp history pertinent to Camp Raritan," n.d.). As did other organizations at the time, Life Camps established a military policy during World War II to pay a partial salary to staff members who were serving in the war, including those who were only seasonal employees. One of these people was J. Millard van Dien, who had worked with the camps for some years. In a letter to Pvt. van Dien during the war, Sharp mentioned that William Gunn, the director of Camp Raritan, and DeAlton Partridge, National Camp staff member and assistant professor from Montclair State Teachers College in New Jersey, were also being paid as part of the Life Camp military policy (Sharp, 1945a). One of the narrators was also stationed in the military and recollected,

> I worked there [at Raritan] from the day I met [L. B.] until the war came. I went into the military. Even when I was in the military, a lot of my assignments were reasonably close to New York City. I would get a leave of absence and I would drive right up to camp and work with the kids. That was my furlough (E. Ambry, personal communication, February 10, 2002).

Faculty at National Camp. Sharp both recruited and drew instructional staff members for the National Camp institutes from around the nation. Most of the faculty members were employed during the year as educators in public or private school systems, including many who were professors in higher education. Some had considerable expertise in their particular field of study.

According to people who knew Sharp, he both influenced and was influenced by these National Camp associates. The narrators often mentioned some of the other staff members at National Camp. For example,

> A terrific staff member at National Camp who was helpful to me was Dr. Phil Walker. I called him the 'walking encyclopedia.' As far as I know right now, he's head of the biology department at Plattsburg College in New York State (C. Emanuelson, personal communication, January 21, 2002).

> Other faculty there [included] 'Moosewood,' who was actually Dr. William Harlow from Syracuse University, the School of Forestry. His book, *Trees in the Eastern United States*, was terrific because it not only gave you the identification, it gave you the history of the tree and . . . how the tree was used (C. Emanuelson, personal communication, January 21, 2002).

> Another one who gave L. B. some influence was William, Dr. Harlow, professor of dendrology of Syracuse University (T. Rillo, personal communication, December 27, 2001).

A most significant and revered National Camp staff member was William "Cap'n Bill" Vinal. Sharp became acquainted with Vinal early in his career through camp leadership courses taught at Teachers College – Columbia University. Years before, as a young man, Vinal had been the head of the Nature Guide Service at Yosemite National Park in California. Vinal studied botany at Harvard University and was later a faculty member at several colleges. He was widely published on the topics of botany, nature study, and camping education. At the time he met Sharp, he was teaching at Massachusetts State College at Amherst. He had been very much involved in the American Nature Study Society since 1911, and was still active in 1957 ("Salute to Cap'n Bill," 1957). From 1939 until 1945, he taught at National Camp as the primary naturalist. The relationship between Sharp and Vinal is well-documented through personal letters between the two men that are held in the special collections at Southern Illinois University, Carbondale.

In August of 1945, Vinal informed Sharp through a letter that he and his wife would not be returning to National Camp in the following summers to work, although he still planned to be involved with Life Camp and National Camp endeavors. He wrote, "As you know, I believe in your philosophy to the nth degree. . . . I'll be glad to join in on indoctrination trips. . . . Our very best wishes go to you in your crusade. We are 100% for you and the effort" (Vinal, 1945, p. 1–2). Sharp responded with an emotional letter saying that he suspected Vinal's leaving when he noticed a Johnny Appleseed costume and other items missing at the end of the camp season. Sharp complained, "Little do you know of the real difficulties I have to face this year. . . . We are not over the hump. It will be harder this year" (Sharp, 1945b, p. 1). He wrote that he could not "replace you two ever" (p. 2). Several narrators mentioned the relationship between Vinal and Sharp. A few of them recounted,

> Somebody else who had a great impact on him was Captain Bill Vinal. That may have been the most significant . . . person of influence on L. B. That goes back into the teens and early '20s. That relationship was a very, very critical one (R. Christie, personal communication, May 9, 2002).

> Captain Bill, who was a professor of nature education at the University of Massachusetts in Amherst, developed a Socratic method of teaching in the outdoors. The Socratic method was not giving the answer but instead asking penetrating questions, leading questions, where the learner begins to learn on his or her own by [a] hands-on type of sensitivity, gathering the facts through the senses. He was a master teacher. He was a great influence on L. B. Sharp in terms of how L. B. taught in the out-of-doors. Captain Bill Vinal was also on the National Camp staff (T. Rillo, personal communication, December 27, 2001).

L. B. certainly had an understanding of the world about him. He made sure all of the teachers at National were the best to be had [such as] Cap'n Bill from the University of Massachusetts, the first school to put 'Nature Study' into a department, and people who understood leadership (E. Roller, personal communication, January 28, 2002).

In the years after the opening of National Camp in 1940, several key events took place in outdoor education. Exemplary programs were developed based on National Camp philosophies. New facilities were constructed. Graduates of National Camp started their own programs or joined in on the efforts of other outdoor organizations. Many of them published articles and books on outdoor education. These pivotal events led to what eventually was referred to as the outdoor education movement.

— 3 —

Growth of the Movement (1940s)

In the years after the opening of National Camp in 1940, several scattered but significant events took place in education in the outdoors. Numerous educational programs and facilities were developed, often by graduates of National Camp who started their own initiatives or joined in on the efforts of other organizations. Not only was there tremendous definition and expansion of the outdoor education movement during the 1940s, but funding challenges also emerged. This chapter highlights several of the pivotal events that occurred during that time period.

Extending Education

The first issue of *Extending Education* (1944) was published by Life Camps, Inc. in January of 1944. The purpose for the publication was to offer monographs pertaining to dimensions of outdoor education and to feature "outstanding examples" (Sharp, 1944, p. 1) of programs and projects that extended education into the outdoors. An additional purpose of *Extending Education* identified by Sharp was "to do everything possible to extend what we believe to be the education of the future" (p. 1). The last edition of the publication was dated in 1961, and was published from Carbondale, Illinois, where Sharp had relocated just a year earlier (*Extending Education*, 1961).

Camp Woodland Springs, Salesmanship Club

Around 1946 Sharp was hired to survey and provide consultation services for a new summer camp to be built by the Salesmanship Club near Dallas, Texas, for "underprivileged" boys (Sharp, 1946a, p. 23). Based on Sharp's recommendations, the new camp was named Camp Woodland Springs. Campbell Loughmiller, a National Camp graduate, was hired as the first director of the camp and implemented many National Camp practices into the Woodland Springs program.

Cliff Emanuelson, who had been a National Camp student and staff member, also worked at Camp Woodland Springs in later years. He recollected,

> I graduated [from Springfield College] in 1950. Then . . . I went to Camp Woodland Springs, which [was] a camp for boys, fed upon the same system as National Camp. There were other staff members there that I had met at National. . . . I went there [to work] with youngsters that had difficulty and had a choice of going to camp or going to reform school. They were pretty eager to go to camp instead. [They were] always cooking at least two [of the] day's meals every day or going on a camping trip, a canoe trip, covered wagon trip, similar to what we did at National Camp (C. Emanuelson, personal communication, January 21, 2002).

It is not clear if Sharp was the connection who brought Loughmiller and Salesmanship Club together, or if Loughmiller specifically went to National Camp in preparation for his upcoming position with Salesmanship Club. The latter may be likely since he had been involved with social agencies in the Dallas area (Loughmiller, 1965). However, Sharp's (1946a) report does stress that professional leadership would be needed that was "equal to that needed

for the principalship of a high school and the salary commensurate with that position. The director should have qualifications for educational administration and leadership, and in addition special ability and preparation for directing the camp program" (p. 25). Sharp's comments were based on a vision for the camp to operate full-time in the summer and then year-round on weekends. The camp soon expanded into a residential, year-round program for at-risk boys due to the successful progress made by campers who were "possibly emotionally disturbed" (Loughmiller, 1965, p. v). Plans were discussed and piloted for specifically serving boys whose "difficulties required treatment outside the home" (p. v). The new program began in November of 1946 with one group of eight boys and two counselors. By the following summer, the program had grown to 40 boys and 10 counselors (Loughmiller, 1947).

Loughmiller directed Camp Woodland Springs for several years, and went on to develop a therapeutic model there that gave birth to wilderness adventure therapy and still serves today as the foundational philosophy for the National Association of Therapeutic Wilderness Camps. That particular site for Camp Woodland Springs was used until 1957, when the city encroached too much, and the camp was relocated to Hawkins, Texas, about 90 miles east of Dallas. Sharp was also involved in these later endeavors, serving as a consultant while Salesmanship Club was considering new properties and expansion opportunities (Loughmiller, 1954). The Salesmanship Club served as a model for numerous wilderness therapy programs across the United States. Unfortunately, the Club closed its therapeutic camping program in 2003 after nearly six decades of operation (Journal of Therapeutic Wilderness Camping, 2004, p. 49).

Julian Smith and the W. K. Kellogg Foundation

In the early 1940s the W. K. Kellogg Foundation began to operate outdoor educational programs at two of its facilities near Battle Creek, Michigan. The facilities were St. Mary's Lake Camp and Clear Lake Camp. Julian Smith, also recognized as an early pioneer in outdoor education, was a school administrator from a nearby county and served on the board of directors for the Kellogg outdoor programs. By 1945 Smith had been hired by the Michigan State Department of Public Instruction and was also involved in a joint five-year study with Western Michigan University and the Kellogg Foundation's work with outdoor education (Elliott & Smith, 1947).

Around that time the Kellogg camps began to draw attention toward Michigan as a potential hot spot for outdoor educational programming, as evidenced by numerous correspondences between Sharp and others. Sharp received a letter from Julian Smith (1947) that stated, "So many things are happening and so fast that I feel the need of some fatherly advice from you" (p. 1). Don Hammerman, an early staff member with the Kellogg camps, offered the following explanations of the formative years as outdoor education programming became concentrated at the Clear Lake site:

> Leslie Clark had been George Donaldson's assistant director at St. Mary's Lake Camp. George Donaldson was the director of the . . . program at St. Mary's. George was then hired to go down to Tyler, Texas, and direct [a new outdoor education program there]. Les moved over [to Clear Lake Camp] from St. Mary's. . . . Les Clark had been a National Camper, so I'm sure some of the elements of the Clear Lake program probably emanated from National Camps, from their outlook on camping education. There were cookouts, for example. There was an emphasis on some of the outdoor living skills, as well as relating to the content areas of the curriculum, and purposeful work experiences. That was all a part of the Michigan outlook, too. That was also a part of National Camps, to be engaged in purposeful work (D. Hammerman, personal communication, January 6, 2002).

> At that time, as I recall, there were only three year-round school camps in the nation. One was Clear Lake. The other two were in California, Camp High Hill and Cuyamaca (D. Hammerman, personal communication, January 6, 2002).

Clear Lake Camp was the location for some significant early conferences and meetings on outdoor education. The same narrator described his recollections of first meeting L. B. Sharp at a conference held at there.

> My first direct face-to-face meeting with L. B. was at Clear Lake while I was still there between '51 and '54 at the National Conference sponsored by the Michigan Department of Public Instruction and the W. K. Kellogg Foundation. That was the summer of '52. People were invited in from all over

the country. Most of them were in higher education. They really weren't the practitioners. In fact, it really was directed toward teacher education. L. B. was there as one of the key-noters or significant consultants for the conference. . . . The conference planners prevailed upon L. B. to lead a vesper service for which he was known. . . . [H]e led one at Clear Lake down by the lakeside. It was very inspirational, tying in the fire and the flame and the meaning of all this (D. Hammerman, personal communication, January 6, 2002).

The program at Clear Lake, later named the Battle Creek Outdoor School Laboratory, is still in operation today. Hammerman commented on the influences on the students and staff members who participated in the programs there.

Clear Lake served as a training ground for many people who left to assume leadership positions in California, Texas, Ohio, Illinois, the east coast. They went all over the country, and some remained in outdoor education for the duration of their careers (D. Hammerman, personal communication, January 6, 2002).

More Changes in Terminology

During these years, differentiation was beginning to be established between school camping or residential outdoor education and outdoor education that did not necessarily involve being away from the school site. The following describes Don Hammerman's perspective of the development of outdoor education during the 1940s and the years beyond:

I saw three changes in terminology. I think the first reference to educational camping was the one Sharp used: 'camping education,' camping that was educational. Some of the early experiments in camping education, and even some of the early experiments in school camping, took place primarily during summertime. Then, there was a gradual transition . . . and the recognition that if this is a worthwhile endeavor for educational institutions to engage in, why not do it on school time? That's when the literature and the terminology began to change. We began to refer to it not as camping education but as 'school camping,' camping engaged in by schools and on school time. Still the emphasis was pretty much on camping-type skills. Then there was a gradual growing away from camp-type activities to a closer connection with ongoing curriculum—what was happening in schools and trying to reinforce what was happening in the classroom by means of the firsthand experience in the out-of-doors. Then, sometime between '57 and '61 . . . John Hug, who was on our staff at Taft Campus. . . . came up with the term 'resident outdoor education.' He's the first one that I know of who coined [that specific] term. His thinking was, well, there's outdoor learning that takes place on school grounds, or in various outdoor settings. But then there's that kind of outdoor education that takes place in a resident setting, not necessarily in camps. He was the one who said, 'Why not call it resident outdoor education?' There are short-term outdoor education experiences and then there's the longer term or resident outdoor experience. Gradually, that term began to infiltrate the literature. When I heard L. B. use the term once or twice, 'resident outdoor education,' rather than school camping, I knew we had arrived (D. Hammerman, personal communication, January 6, 2002).

Editor of the Bulletin of the NASSP

Hugh Masters was an educator involved with the W. K. Kellogg Foundation in Michigan and its early work in outdoor education. In transcripts of a conversation between Sharp and Masters, Sharp (1946b) stated,

> The meeting was the best I have ever attended dealing with Camping and Outdoor Education. That is quite a statement. They all wanted to know about it and how they should go about it. I think Michigan is the 'red hot' spot in this country.

I am revising this plan we were talking of. The first place we start should be in Michigan (p. 1).

The phrase *Camping and Outdoor Education* used by Sharp above referred to the name of the May 1947 issue of the *Bulletin of the National Association of Secondary School Principals*. Sharp and DeAlton Partridge, who was the associate director of Life Camps and National Camp in 1947, were the guest editors for the issue. Paul E. Elicker (1947), the executive editor of the *Bulletin*, wrote,

> Cognizant of the importance of this kind of education for our youth, the National Association of Secondary School Principals eagerly sought a descriptive account of the growth and effectiveness of camping and outdoor education from the distinguished national leader in this area of education for youth, Dr. L. B. Sharp (p. 7).

Narrator Ed Ambry offered the following recollections pertaining to Sharp's editorship of the *Bulletin*:

> They invited L. B. Sharp—they sort of commandeered him. . . . Almost anybody that knew anything about outdoor education wrote articles. . . . This was an association that got excited about what L. B. Sharp was talking about and asked him to do a complete publication. . . . It took a long time to put together. . . . It was a great push for L. B. Sharp's philosophy (E. Ambry, personal communication, February 10, 2002).

> There were a lot of people who wrote about what he knew about, especially in this "Camping and Outdoor Education" publication. Everybody and anybody who knew L. B. Sharp wrote an article in that (E. Ambry, personal communication, February 10, 2002).

Changes in Marital Status

It appeared that Sharp and his wife, Alice, probably separated in the spring of 1947, as he penned a letter to her in March of that year talking of the splitting of their finances. In the letter, Sharp (1947) gave birthday greetings to Alice, and thanked her for her recent birthday card to him.

A few of the narrators commented briefly on Sharp's divorce and admitted that they did not know the details of the situation. Most of them met L. B. years afterward and did not know his wife or daughter. Clifford Knapp suggested,

> He didn't have much of a family connection because he was divorced. . . . I don't know the story of why he was distant from his daughter, but there didn't seem to be much of a family connection at all. His extended family, then, consisted of the people who he gathered around in his work. And so, I became kind of an adopted son for a year, although he never called me that. I just felt that (C. Knapp, personal communication, December 19, 2001).

The New Jersey State School of Conservation

In 1949, the New Jersey State School of Conservation (NJSSC), regulated by Montclair State College, opened a residential outdoor education program for college students and children near Branchville, New Jersey (Pons, 1958). The children's camp, known as Camp Wapalanne, was located on Lake Wapalanne. The following narrative tells of the establishment of the new program at NJSSC:

> When I was an undergraduate at Panzer College, which was a small specialization school for physical education, Panzer was an outstanding school. We would have camping institutes built into our freshman and sophomore year. The institutes had moved when I was a freshman after service in 1948 to the NJSSC that had just opened up. It had lain dormant for ten years. . . . I met [L. B.] for a second time because he

came to speak to the Panzer students. . . . Panzer students were the first group to utilize the facilities. We were also the first group of students to sweep out the cabins, and sweep out the leaves, and carry the beds up to the cabins, and open up the place which had remained basically unoccupied for ten years. The camp was just located about four miles, five miles, from Life Camps. . . . Some of our cooks came from L. B.'s camp to work at the School of Conservation (T. Rillo, personal communication, December 27, 2001).

NJSSC was created as a co-sponsored project of the New Jersey State Department of Education and the Department of Conservation and Economic Development. The school was developed for the joint purpose of serving as a teacher demonstration site for conservation and as a conservation program for school children. Based on the principles of National Camp, the NJSSC program concentrated on the issues of food, shelter, and self-occupation (Pons, 1958). Edward Ambry (1954), a Montclair faculty member and the director of NJSSC in 1954, described many of the program practices used at the school as originating from Sharp and National Camp. In addition to Sharp, DeAlton Partridge and Edward Ambry were instrumental in the original formation of NJSSC, both of whom had been graduates from National Camp (Rosebrock, 1961).

Four of the narrators became associated with Sharp through their relationship to the NJSSC. They shared the following stories:

I went there [to Montclair State College] as a professor in 1951. I stayed there 28 years. I taught psychology, child psychology, and some education courses. Part of my assignment was to run [the] camp that was in New Jersey that was part of Montclair State College. I did that for five years, and then [Cliff] Emanuelson took over that job. That was when I was appointed the dean of the graduate school (E. Ambry, personal communication, February 10, 2002).

[I] went to teach after my master's at Ridgewood, New Jersey. Fortunately, I hit it right off with the superintendent because he was from San Diego and San Diego was into [school] camping for years by that time. . . . [I asked,] 'Do you think you might want to have a school camping program here at Ridgewood?' He said, 'Yes. . . . You can take the sixth grade class. We'll work on it and see if you can't go out as a model program for the one year.' We ended up taking two classes to the New Jersey State School of Conservation, which was an offshoot from National Camp in New Jersey. . . . Ed Ambry, by that time, was the acting director for the School of Conservation through Montclair. . . . The third year, we took all of the sixth grade classes. It got to where [the superintendent was] hiring people for the sixth grade classes. They would hire people with the understanding they were going to camp (C. Emanuelson, personal communication, January 21, 2002).

When I was working to get this thing started in Ridgewood, I called [L. B.] and told him I was having a meeting with the parents for the first class to go out from Ridgewood. He showed up right there in the meeting. Here I was sweating, but he and Ed Ambry showed up at that meeting. So, I introduced him and he said a few words, and he wished us all the luck in the world. In fact, he came to visit us at camp, too. Wherever he could, he would do his best to help you out and move you along (C. Emanuelson, personal communication, January 21, 2002).

[Three years later], I was offered a position as director of the New Jersey State School of Conservation. I worked there for five years. L. B. Sharp was only about five miles away in the summer time. . . . Whenever he would visit, we would use him (C. Emanuelson, personal communication, January 21, 2002).

By working as a counselor at the New Jersey State School of Conservation in the summer time, I began to go over to Life Camps. Ed Ambry became the director of the New Jersey School of Conservation, and he . . . employed me to work [there] (T. Rillo, personal communication, December 27, 2001).

I went to Paterson State College [in New Jersey], and I studied to be a junior high school educator. . . . It was in 1958 when I took a course called 'Camping Education.' . . . We went on a weekend field trip to the New Jersey School of Conservation . . . in Branchville where I saw that you could actually have a profession called outdoor education (C. Knapp, personal communication, December 19, 2001).

L. B. Sharp was located across the Delaware River in Matamoras, Pennsylvania, at Pole Bridge Camp at that time. I applied for a camp counselor job that following summer after I discovered the NJSSC. Then, as a part of a counselor training session, we went across the Delaware River to Pennsylvania and met L. B. Sharp. . . . He was talking to the whole group, and I heard a strange sound in the woods. I figured it was a bird, and I said, 'L. B., what's that bird?' and he said, 'Why don't you go and find out?' This was so typical of L. B. because he wouldn't easily give you answers when he thought you could find out yourself. Even if you couldn't easily find out yourself, he was opposed to giving you an answer. I couldn't believe that he was asking me to leave the group. He was lecturing. So, I did and I found that it was a Yellow-billed Cuckoo, a new bird to me. That was my first really powerful introduction to L. B. Sharp on that visit in 1958 (C. Knapp, personal communication, December 19, 2001).

Outdoor Teacher Education at Northern Illinois University

Leslie Holmes, the president of Northern Illinois State Teachers College, later named Northern Illinois University (NIU), began implementing plans in 1951 to renovate buildings on land that had once been the art center for sculptor Lorado Taft. The site was developed by Holmes for teacher preparation in outdoor education and named the Lorado Taft Field Campus. The first director there was Paul Harrison, who was appointed in 1954. Donald Hammerman, a narrator for this study and a former staff member from the Clear Lake Camp in Michigan, was appointed as the educational director in 1954 and the director in 1965. Hammerman also served for some years as the head of the Department of Outdoor Teacher Education at NIU. He retired from the field campus in 1979 (Knapp, 1991). Hammerman offered the following insights into the beginning of the Lorado Taft Field Campus and Sharp's involvement there:

> The designing [of the field campus] was almost a happenstance kind of thing. Some of the buildings were already in existence, quarried from a local quarry right there on the bluff, by the artists of limestone and dolomite. We kept three of the original three or four buildings. The others were just torn down and some new structures built. There was really no grand master plan at the time. . . . We just created it, but the strong influences there would have been, I would say, the Michigan philosophy of outdoor education and what I'd been inculcated with while I was there at Clear Lake during three years, plus everything I had assimilated from reading L. B. and Julian Smith and whoever else (D. Hammerman, personal communication, January 6, 2002).

Not only did the Lorado Taft Field Campus become an integral component for teacher preparation for NIU and outdoor education experiences for area public school children, but it evolved into a recognized demonstration site for outdoor education across the United States. In 1960, the Field Campus was the host site for the first National Conference in Outdoor Education. The *Journal of Outdoor Education* was established and published through Lorado Taft Field Campus, beginning with the pilot issue in Spring of 1966. George Donaldson was the first editor (*Journal of Outdoor Education*, 1966). Publication apparently ceased after 1994. The Field Campus is still operating today for area school children, although the use of it for teacher preparation was unfortunately ceased in 2000 when NIU's College of Education ended its relationship with the Field Campus (Regional History Center, 2005).

Continued Evolution of National Camp

Throughout the 1940s, outdoor leadership courses at National Camp continued with New York University (NYU), the New Jersey State Colleges, and the New York State Colleges. Toward the end of that decade, changes were occurring that affected some of Sharp's endeavors in expanding the work of Life Camps and National Camps.

Early framing of an outdoor education association. Although Sharp had received the memo nearly two years earlier stating Time, Inc.'s intentions to cease or decrease funding for Life Camps and National Camp, this severing had not yet occurred by February of 1946, when Sharp (1946c) wrote to Roy Larsen, one of the Time, Inc. executives. Sharp told Larsen of the many male campers and counselors who had been returning from their war service in the military and had come to the Life Camps office in New York. Sharp claimed that most of them had come to the office within twelve hours of arriving back in New York. He wrote, "Life Camps has meant far more to them than we ever realized" (p. 1). Sharp included a poem in his memo written by a soldier and ex-Life Camper about coming across the burning French town of Martincourt that had been destroyed by the German Nazis.

In 1948 or 1949, a lengthy proposal was drafted for Life Camps and NYU to join forces and fund-raising capabilities in order to create a national outdoor education organization and to establish an outdoor education center at NYU. The purpose of the proposed organization was to expand the work of National Camp outdoor leadership training to a national scale. In a letter to the vice-chancellor at NYU, Sharp (1949a) claimed, "It would be the only center in the United States where this kind of leadership preparation is given" (p. 1).

In March of 1949, Sharp wrote to C. D. Jackson, vice-president of Time, Inc. and chairman of the Life Camp board of directors, and to Francis Pratt, an executive at Time, Inc. In the letter, Sharp explained that a group of people had met to discuss the NYU proposal and had determined to proceed with formation of the proposed national organization. Representatives from Life Camps, NYU, and from some other related entities would form an organization called the Outdoor Education Foundation or Outdoor Education, Inc. This organization would begin negotiations with NYU to establish a center for outdoor education (Sharp, 1949b). It is not clear if the new center was originally intended to be located at NYU or National Camp in Pennsylvania, as Sharp mentioned that changes to

the proposal were in the process of being made because NYU could not legally own or operate property outside of New York State.

That same summer in 1949, a brochure from NYU advertised summer session outdoor leadership courses at Lake Sebago Interstate Park in Sloatsburg, New York. The courses were coordinated by Jay B. Nash, a professor in the School of Education at NYU. Some of the courses were taught by Sharp and listed as being offered in cooperation with National Life Camps at Sussex, New Jersey. Some of these courses were "Science and Camping Education," "Camp Administration and Leadership," and "Guidance in Group-Living Situations" (New York University, 1949).

By June of 1950, National Camp had been relocated directly across the Delaware River from Camp Pole Bridge, which was situated on the Pennsylvania side of the river near Matamoras. The new National Camp held its official address as Port Jervis, New York. It would appear that this move was an attempted remedy for NYU's inability to own property outside of New York.

Integrated staff at Life Camps. Life Camps had become racially integrated in the early 1940s when they began to enroll African-American children as campers. However, the instructional staff remained non-integrated until the end of that decade. The following narrative by Larry Huntley describes what was involved in the first steps taken toward the racial integration of staff members.

> [Near] the end of '49 . . . Bill [Gunn, the director at Raritan], had announced that they had never had a black person on the counseling staff. Black kids . . . but never a black counselor. They wanted to begin integrating the camp staff. Well, I think about six of us signed up for it. I [was] thinking the other day how Bill Gunn might have determined [why I] was to be the one. It struck me that the probability was that I had been assigned to Hill Tepee. . . . He had thought that was the best age level for the new counselor to be, rather than the very young boys or the older ones. And so, he picked the age group rather

than pick the counselor, but he did have to have a counselor who had agreed to be the co-counselor. . . . The older boys might have a little more prejudice. The younger ones might have wild comments or whatever. The middle age [was] kind of blasé, take it as it comes, and they did—never a problem (L. Huntley, personal communication, March 15, 2002).

Challenges at the crossroads. In the fall of 1950, Sharp received a letter from Ernest Melby, the Dean of Education at NYU, informing Sharp that cooperative arrangements between NYU and National Camp for summer leadership sessions had been discontinued. That announcement was confirmed by another letter to Sharp dated the same day from Jay B. Nash (1950), chair of the Department of Physical Education, Health, and Recreation at NYU, who stated, "You are, of course, familiar with the fact that Life Camps, Inc. and New York University have reached a stalemate in regard to the cooperative plan of training camp leaders" (no page). Nash mentioned that credit recognition for courses given outside the university would no longer be provided.

Lois Goodrich (1951), the director of the Girls' Camp still located at Lake Mashipacong near Sussex, New Jersey, sent a memo to Sharp and William Gunn, the director at Camp Raritan entitled, "Lois' vote for our future" (p. 1). She explained that she had been considering all of the proposed plans and that her thoughts at the time were to go with what she referred to as "Plan 4—To run the children's camps, close National, and do field service only" (p. 1), meaning speeches, articles, surveys, consultation, films, and special institutes held around the country. She also suggested year-round residential living at the children's camps, as she talked of having nine campers at each of the three Life Camps and getting some funding from a youth board agency in the amount of $90 per month per child. Goodrich addressed her thoughts regarding the outdoor education movement, stating,

If we had more money, we could continue this project and cause outdoor education to advance more rapidly. It will advance, inevitably, however, without us, with the start we have given it. . . . To feel that we are abandoning 'the Movement' in so doing [by closing National Camp] is giving ourselves the lie. It has begun; it is under way; it will not die (p. 1).

Goodrich (1951) claimed that an accurate estimate of 85% of past staff members had gone into working with youth, mostly in educational institutions. The following narrative segments provide some detailed information surrounding the changes that were about to happen at National Camp:

It was at this time L. B. Sharp came to a crossroads of his career. There was some dissention, especially at Girls' Camp at Mashipacong. . . . Somehow Life and Time Incorporated were convinced that they were going down the wrong path, that they shouldn't be doing teacher education. They should concentrate on the poor kids in New York City. So they withdrew their support. L. B. Sharp relocated at that time to Pole Bridge (T. Rillo, personal communication, December 27, 2001).

After the war, the Time and Life Corporation decided that they did not want to finance this relatively small concept. They wanted to build a series of international camps around the world to help poor countries and other people through outdoor education, but they wanted to do it their way. L. B. Sharp had different ideas, and so he left Time and Life Corporation (E. Ambry, personal communication, February 10, 2002).

When L. B. left the Time and Life Corporation, the family that owned [Time-Life] gave him a bonus when he left and arranged for him to fly around the world. There was no bitterness in his leaving. What he wanted to do and what they wanted to do were two different things. And that was the beginning of the end of any kind of big money (E. Ambry, personal communication, February 10, 2002).

— 4 —
Endings and New Beginnings (1950s)

The Creation of the Outdoor Education Association

In a series of letters written in 1951 to Reynold Carlson and other close associates to enlist their help with the National Camp institutes, Sharp announced a monetary contribution that had been made to continue the efforts of National Camp. To Carlson, he wrote, "A new name will have to be decided immediately. . . . This good news now removes any screen of uncertainty about immediate plans and we will want to go full steam ahead" (Sharp, 1951a, p. 1).

The Outdoor Education Association (OEA) was subsequently established with the help of friends during 1951 or 1952 after moving National Camp to the Pole Bridge Camp site in Pennsylvania (Piercy, 1978). Once National Camp was re-established there, Pole Bridge operated as a camp for both girls and boys, under the management of the OEA and was no longer affiliated with Life Camps (Outdoor Education Association, 1955). Ed Ambry played a part in the beginning of the OEA and explained,

> [In forming the OEA] we had a committee of about 15 people.
> . . . [OEA] started when L. B. Sharp was still in New York. It

was known [at first] as the National Outdoor Education Association. For years, I was the treasurer (E. Ambry, personal communication, February 10, 2002).

Partial plans for raising funds to operate the OEA were for Sharp and the association to offer consultation services in outdoor education. Sharp conducted survey work and master planning and design for future outdoor education sites. Some comments regarding Sharp's consultation work follow:

> The Outdoor Education Association was an attempt to make money to support [the camps]. The money wasn't coming in like it used to and it was up to L. B. Sharp to go out and do his own personal fund raising, which he did by doing camp surveys. These camp surveys, many of them were [for] church camps (T. Rillo, personal communication, December 27, 2001).

> [For his consultation work, L. B.] spoke into the dictaphone and then he had his secretary transcribe. He would rework that text, but then he would fit it into a template developed for other master plans. Many of his master plans, I'm sure, had many of the same paragraphs just pulled from one to the other, because that was his way of promoting the decentralized camping philosophy (C. Knapp, personal communication, December 19, 2001).

Closing of Life Camps

Finally in 1953, a formal announcement of the closing of Life Camps was mass-mailed to alumni and associates, with a plea for contributions to continue the work of the camps under the new name of Trail Blazer Camps. The letter stated, "Life Camps, by that name, are no more" (Pratt, 1953, p. 2). The camps were to be managed by St. John's Guild, an agency that had served disabled and underprivileged children in the New York area since 1866. The announcement was written by Francis Pratt, who referred to herself as the "President of Life Camps and now Trail Blazer Camps" (Pratt, 1953, p. 2). Pratt was also one of the Time, Inc. executives who had been involved with the Life Camps for some years (Time, Inc., 1944).

A following letter was written by Lois Goodrich (1953), the director of what was previously the Girls' Camp, and sent to past Life Camp staff members in June of 1953 as an appeal for contributions. Goodrich mentioned that the Life Camps had been struggling to continue operation over the previous few years.

On the same day that the Pratt (1953) letter was written, Philip Walker (1953), a former Camp Raritan, Pole Bridge Camp, and National Camp staff member, wrote an emotionally charged letter to Sharp. Walker had recently received a letter that had been sent to former Life Camp campers and counselors telling of the closing of Life Camps. Walker did not name the author of the letter he received, but was in strong disagreement with the author's claim that the closing of Life Camps was due to "a too-ambitious program for national expansion and emphasis on other than children's camps which brought about a financial collapse of everything" (p. 1). Walker protested the letter, calling it a "nefarious attempt at subterfuge and half truths" (p. 1), and lauded Sharp for his accomplishments over the years. Walker stated his views that Sharp had

> practically single-handed[ly] sold [his] idea to the people who made it possible . . . and then skyrocketed it to the whole country and world by careful prodigious programming and tireless planning into the most promising, meaningful, challenging and evident solution to the educational dilemma in this country than any recent movement in education (p. 1).

Walker (1953) signed the letter with the phrase in quotations, "Never finished. Just begun" (p. 2), a common phrase used at National and Life Camps.

Recollections from Girl's Camp at Lake Mashipacong. A few of the narrators who had worked or spent time at the camp offered some of their memorable experiences in the following descriptions:

> [There was a] quaking bog. I'd been at this bog near Lake Mashipacong with Cap'n Vinal and also with L. B. You would jump up and down and these big trees go up and down with you. . . . The lake is being reclaimed and sphagnum moss and the roots of plants have caused a mat. If you jump up and down, the whole thing goes up and down. The trees are maybe twelve to sixteen inches and they're going up and down, shaking like mad, so you do the bog trot. L. B. Sharp was good at the bog trot. He had more animation than Captain Bill at the bog trot. There were all kinds of plants that were very typical of Labrador up in northern New Jersey. This was a wonderful laboratory adjacent to National Camp and so we'd always take a trip (T. Rillo, personal communication, December 27, 2001).

> They had a sawmill where they milled their own logs and built their own buildings. Millard van Dien was the chief foreman. . . . He became L. B. Sharp's chief maintenance man, caretaker, builder, construction person, you name it. Millard van Dien was a unique product of rural New York state from Port Jervis with an infinite number of skills, construction skills, woodcraft skills. They developed a shelter called a 'Shadien.' S-h-a- for Sharp, D-i-e-n for Dien, a shadien. . . . Millard was with [L. B.] until he moved to Pole Bridge and then Millard became chief maintenance person at the New Jersey State School of Conservation. . . . L. B. Sharp used to depend on him for many of the constructions. They built 'Single Tree' and 'Double Tree.' Single Tree was the library. Double Tree [was] the office, the administration building. . . . We had the lumberjack theme, the lumbering theme as well as the Native American theme running together in some of the names of the buildings. Every small group had a name that they gave themselves (T. Rillo, personal communication, December 27, 2001).

[L. B.] invented, with the caretaker of the camp, a type of shelter. It was called a 'Shadien,' but it was not very practical. I remember him fussing at me when I questioned the usability of it (E. Roller, personal communication, January 28, 2002).

One summer, college presidents from New York and New Jersey came to visit the Life Camps. I remember having the president of NYU . . . [as a] guest for breakfast at my small camp of eight girls and two counselors. The girls had decided on what to cook. The two who were in charge that morning decided to have tomato scrambled eggs. . . . I was a little worried, but it went off well with many questions. I was, at that time, getting my M.A. [master of arts] at NYU—the first in the country in outdoor education. The president of NYU offered me a job that morning. If L. B. could get people like that interested in outdoor education, he could get anyone to try it! (E. Roller, personal communication, January 28, 2002).

Although it was written years before the closing of Life Camps, a letter written to Sharp by a Girls' Camp camper is indicative of the meaningful experiences derived there. She wrote, "We learned to lash and nail, to saw and split with a true woodsman's eye. We dug and chopped and lifted and what was more, we did those things together, shoulder to shoulder" (Goodrich, 1939, p. 1). The girl claimed she was "very grateful for having had a chance to see the new Life Camp in its early stages and to be a small part of something so big that it takes my breath away sometimes to think of it" (p. 2). She further stated, "The whole idea of the Village and each part of it, like the Store and Chimney Corner, is splendid. It gives just the right spirit of Unity to camp and still preserves the individuality of each small camp" (p. 2).

Recollections from Camp Raritan. The property at Raritan was located near Pottersville, New Jersey, the furthest south of the three Life Camps. Raritan had begun operation as one of *Life*'s Camps for boys in 1923 (Sharp, 1930). Larry Huntley and Tom Rillo, who had worked at Camp Raritan, shared their recollections below:

> [L. B.] always came down to camp at the end of the season. . . . That was one of the highlights that helped keep everybody there. And it was a real treat. It was a treat to meet L. B. and experience [a coal-roasted steak dinner called a buffalo throw] and just to rub shoulders with him as we had dinner afterward. He spent the day there. It was just kind of a bonus. We didn't get paid all that much. Getting to know L. B. was quite significant (L. Huntley, personal communication, March 15, 2002).

> We had planned an all day hike. In advance, we laid out our program at the beginning of the month, and we suggested this possibility, that we would prepare all of the food the day before, and dig a pit and get the proper greenery brush to cover it. We had a Dutch oven and all the ingredients for our evening dinner. . . . We planned steak, vegetables, potatoes, onions. . . . We started the pit fire the night before to get a good bed of hardwood coals. We had it protected against any fire hazard overnight. That's standard practice. In the morning, we had all of our dinner in the Dutch oven. We set it in the pit right on the coals, covered it with leafy greenery that wouldn't catch fire and just piled it on to keep the heat in and we went off on our hike (L. Huntley, personal communication, March 15, 2002).

> When we came back about 4:00, it was raining and it had been raining for a while. But we had a great bunch of kids. We had to walk through the village up to our campsite, and we decided we were going to go in singing. So we picked a couple of songs, and we just sang as we hiked through the village and passed some camp sites up to our own. . . . When we got up to camp, Hill Tepee, . . . the boys' beds were washed downhill to the edge of the tents because they hadn't dug the pit on the upside deep enough. Dinner was awash. As we opened the Dutch oven up, it was a pit of water. . . . So, there was a debate as to what to do. We decided that we would

wash the food off with clean water and cook it and those that wanted to eat it could eat it and the others could eat out of the chuck box, peanut butter and jelly sandwiches and whatever else we had around. I think most of us ate the main dinner, but it was skimpy and by this time it was dark, but it was an experience I don't think many of us would forget. The kids put it down as one of their highlights (L. Huntley, personal communication, March 15, 2002).

The campsite, Hill Tepee, was [for] twelve year olds. One of our campers was, I think, eleven. He was the head of the toughest gang in the area of New York City where he lived. All the other boys, fourteen, fifteen, sixteen, whatever, this eleven year old boy was the head of that gang, using 'gang' in the negative sense. Well, the operation at Raritan, his first year's experience there, turned that kid around. We got the feedback the following year. He had gone back to town, notified his gang that they were going to become a group that did things for the community, a positive force in the community. I don't know what they did, clean up empty lots or whatever, but they were going to turn from what they had been doing into a positive force in the community. That was strictly out of that boy's one month's experience at Raritan (L. Huntley, personal communication, March 15, 2002).

[L. B.] encouraged us to be creative. I remember that we also did writing and especially poetry. I write poetry today. . . . I look back at my experience with L. B. as being an inspiration for poetry. He encouraged my poetry writing. He would read it. A lot of it in the early days was about the out-of-doors. I remember Joe Treu, a fellow camper, [who wrote] the poem, 'What is the night? A dark and fearsome thing. Oh no, it's not. It's born of light and hope,' and it goes on. This [was] a ten year old kid from Hell's Kitchen writing poetry and reading it to others (T. Rillo, personal communication, December 27, 2001).

Recollections from Pole Bridge Camp. Although Pole Bridge Camp continued in conjunction with National Camp after Life Camps ceased operations at Lake Mashipacong and Camp Raritan in 1953, recollections from there were equally as descriptive as those given by former staff members of the Life Camps that closed. Some of those memories are presented by Bob Christie and Tom Rillo in the following:

> My wife and I got married in February, and we went down on our honeymoon to New York City. We met L. B. in the elevator going to his office. . . . He was in his 60s at the time and a very warm, gracious individual. My wife said he was a charming individual. Extremely well-mannered. Of course, he had to hug the bride and stuff like that. . . . Both of us were on staff at National Camp. We lived in a tepee that summer. . . . That would have been 1956. . . . That was at Matamoras, Pennsylvania (R. Christie, personal communication, May 9, 2002).

> We had American Chestnut trees in the forest at Matamoras, Pennsylvania. American Chestnut trees at that time had not survived. It was killed off back in the '20s by the blight. There were still trees that were down on the ground that were still intact. There were suckers of trees between there and the route going over to the Conservation Camp in New Jersey at High Point Park. There was an area [that] was several miles long that when you walked through, you were going through American Chestnuts that were up to two, three, four inches in diameters at the most, and then they would die off. L. B. talked a great deal about the significance of the American Chestnut, the heritage of the Chestnut. It's important in the scheme of things, the ecological concepts. . . . He practiced the reverence. You would talk about things, but you have to live it day by day is one of the things he did. You don't have to talk about a whole lot of things (R. Christie, personal communication, May 9, 2002).

> It was here at Pole Bridge in that period of time [in the early 1950s] that L. B. Sharp developed the concept of the outdoor education trailer, the mobile unit. He began to do these travel trailer trips where a group of [eight or] ten youngsters

and two counselors . . . would be on the road. . . . One side was the library side. The other side was the kitchen side. In the middle were all the gear and the duffels and they were just wonderful little camps on wheels (T. Rillo, personal communication, December 27, 2001).

Julian Smith and Evolving Philosophies

Soon after National Camp was relocated from the Girls' Camp to the Camp Pole Bridge site near Matamoras, Pennsylvania, in 1950, Julian Smith from Michigan and Sharp exchanged a few letters discussing visions for outdoor education on a national scale. In one such letter, Sharp asked for Smith's views on the conflict between National Camp and teacher preparation around the country. Sharp was apparently frustrated that universities were reluctant to embrace the National Camp program into their teacher preparation programs. He expressed his desire to provide a forum for outdoor educators to gather nationally (Sharp, 1953).

In a later correspondence, Smith informed Sharp of his involvement with the Outdoor Education Project in Michigan as part of the American Association for Health, Physical Education, and Recreation (AAHPER). The project was initiated for leadership training in outdoor education, specifically in "casting, fishing, shooting and hunting, boating, and the like" (Smith, 1955, p. 1). The concentration by Smith on outdoor sports would later be a point of delineation often made between Smith's *activity approach* and Sharp's *curriculum approach* to outdoor education. However, in Smith's later perspective, the Outdoor Education Project helped to "broaden the concept of the term to include the teaching of skills, attitudes and appreciation necessary for satisfying outdoor pursuits" (Smith, 1973, p. 50). The narrators offered their perspectives of the relationship between Smith and Sharp and their respective philosophies of outdoor education in the following segments:

There were, in the 1940s and early 1950s, two approaches to outdoor education: L. B.'s, the curriculum enrichment out-of-doors, and the other that was teaching sports skills (E. Roller, personal communication, January 28, 2002).

[Smith] was more interested in the . . . recreation kinds of things . . . not the same kind of philosophy that L. B. Sharp had. . . . They were friendly people. They argued with each other, friendly. . . . They both talked with each other. It's just that when L. B. Sharp was talking about [outdoor education], he was talking about living in the out-of-doors and great things. His philosophy of life was different than just recreation in the out-of-doors (E. Ambry, personal communication, February 10, 2002).

Julian [Smith] was an ex-superintendent from Lake View Schools in Michigan, so he was a professional educator to begin with. He was with the Michigan State Department of Public Instruction under Lee Thurston. . . . One of Julian's favorite statements was that outdoor education is a broad umbrella, and there's room for everyone. When different groups used to try to say, 'Well, we belong in outdoor education,' 'Well, no we belong,' [or] 'Well, outdoor education is really our purview and our province,' Julian would say, 'We all belong under this broad umbrella. There's room for all of us in here.' Conservation educators, recreation educators, experiential educators or adventure educators, outdoor educators, environmental educators. There's room for everybody (D. Hammerman, personal communication, January 6, 2002).

[Smith] got involved with the Outdoor Education Project, which was under the auspices of the AAHPER. In fact, he was director of the Outdoor Education Project for a while, operating out of Washington, D.C. To sustain it, they drew money from archery manufacturers, shotgun manufacturers, fishing tackle manufacturers, Coleman stove, things like that, the oudoor recreation people. That's when a few critics began to say, 'Well, Julian has sold outdoor education down the road. The money's tainted.' Julian's response was, 'Yes, it's tainted money. 'Taint enough.' He played it both ways. ... He was using the money to promote the broad concept of learning in the out-of-doors (D. Hammerman, personal communication, January 6, 2002).

I don't think [Sharp and Smith] were best buddies. They respected one another. . . . I think they had . . . a grudging respect for each other. They were friendly rivals. Each one had his own little sphere, not little sphere, large sphere. They had their own agendas and their own following (D. Hammerman, personal communication, January 6, 2002).

I think, when you get into the experiential components of education, you can have difficulty in putting an interpretation on outdoor education, a definition. You have this 'in, for, and about the out-of-doors.' L. B. was saying that those things that we can best learn in the outdoors, we can go outdoors and learn them. Those things we can do inside, we do inside. Taylor . . . and company wanted to change it. They wanted their own definition: in and for the outdoors. . . . Julian Smith and those people were using that definition. Julian Smith came out and he was very much involved in the sports activities more than other aspects of the curriculum. He came out of physical education, and he promoted that area very well. He talked about the other ones, but when you went to his workshops, he did a lot of sports because he was sponsored by Daisy Air Rifle or fishing tackle companies and other people. His workshops . . . were heavily oriented in that direction and L. B.'s were not at all. [L. B.'s] were curricular dealing with math, English, language arts (R. Christie, personal communication, May 9, 2002).

The Growth of Church Camp Leadership

The first documented request for a National Camp leadership session arranged specifically for church camp leaders was apparently made by Isaac Beckes (1949), a representative of the International Council of Religious Education, a Chicago-based interdenominational association. This initial request resulted in a "Special Session for Church Camp Leaders" held at Lake Mashipacong at the end of the summer of 1950, offered in cooperation with the Special Committee on Camps and Conferences of the International Council of Religious Education (National Camp, 1951), a group renamed a few years later as the National Council of Churches. Sharp (1951b) proclaimed, "This is an exceedingly important development as it opens the way to establish and improve camping for the various church groups throughout the country. This group is anxious to go into the small group decentralized plan of camping" (no page). Many of the narrators discussed Sharp's involvement in church camp leadership. A few excerpts are offered below:

> [L. B.] did a great deal for developing church camping. Rather than going out and setting up these little camps and having church services and other things, it might be a better way to get at religion by getting people out and see how the world works and begin to understand the interconnection and work of the forces that makes these things possible. He had been doing this in decentralized camping (R. Christie, personal communication, May 9, 2002).

> Out of all the [National Camp] counselors, there were approximately a dozen who were pre-theological students, anticipating seminary. That was the year that the National Council of Churches persuaded [L. B.] to give a special session of the training that he offered at National Camps for church leaders, designed for them. They had asked him for many years, and he would not cut back by eliminating any of the teachers' programs and so he added a special week-long session or ten days after their regular session. . . . We asked if we . . . could be an observer and hang around for a few days? He welcomed us, so a number of us went. That's where we got a little bit more familiar with the potential of this for the churches because here were some of the top church leaders, sometimes a state conference minister or top office manager, or sometimes it was the head of the camping and con-

NEW YORK UNIVERSITY · SCHOOL OF EDUCATION

camping education

a program designed for

CAMP ADMINISTRATORS · CAMP COUNSELORS

SCHOOL-CAMP PERSONNEL · TEACHERS · GROUP WORKERS

RECREATION LEADERS · AGENCY ADMINISTRATORS

CAMP COMMITTEES

ference department or segment of the church. [This session was] very interdenominational. It was just, for us, a thrilling experience to be able to have two or three days, whatever it was, there at that time (L. Huntley, personal communication, March 15, 2002).

The church camp leadership institutes continued successfully for years to the extent that they were held in locations other than National Camp. Brochures for the institutes held in 1958, for example, offered an eastern session at National Camp and a mid-western session at Bradford Woods Outdoor Education Center near Bloomington, Indiana. The sessions were conducted by Maurice D. "T-Bone" Bone, who was the Pennsylvania chair of the Committee on Camps and Conferences from the National Council of Churches (National Camp, 1958). The 1959 brochures announcing the church leadership institutes listed a third session being planned in western Oregon. This was the first brochure for the church camp leadership courses where Sharp's name was not listed as a consultant for the institutes (National Camp, 1959).

The 1961 summer brochure for the church leadership institutes revealed plans for sessions to be offered at National Camp in Pennsylvania and Indiana with plans for a southwest session in Texas in 1962 (National Camp, 1961). Bone and Sharp had a long-term professional relationship through their work with church camp leadership.

Another associate of Sharp who worked intensively with church camp leadership was Rodney Britten. Britten was involved with a group of church camp leaders in a book writing project. The proposed book, named *Campsite Selection and Development*, was heavily and humorously critiqued by Sharp. In the report he sent to Britten regarding the text, one objection Sharp stated pertained to the use of the term "outdoor education" in the book's subtitle, *The Church Plans for Outdoor Education* (Sharp, 1963a). Sharp promoted outdoor education as an extension of the school curriculum, and not simply as education that takes places in the outdoors

86

as proposed in the book. An earlier letter from Sharp to Edward Ambry also expressed Sharp's concern over the use of the subtitle since his name was to be designated as a consultant for the book (Sharp, 1963b).

Significant Legislation in New Jersey

In May of 1956, the New Jersey State Board of Education passed legislation, authored by Edward Ambry (n.d.), that required all university sophomores in teacher preparation programs to attend one week in a residential outdoor education experience. The programs were implemented in the spring of 1957 and held at Camp Wapalanne at the New Jersey State School of Conservation. The following narratives comment on this significant endeavor in outdoor education on a state-wide level:

> Politically, we were able to get the state board of education to approve a law that I drafted and eventually passed through the legislature that made it mandatory for every [sophomore] who graduated through the teacher education program to spend one week at the camp at Sussex County. . . . I had a couple of friends in the legislature, . . . and they got it put through. . . . As the population grew, it got to the point where we didn't have enough resources for them, so it became optional again. . . . We did that as a mandatory thing for several years, but then it just wasn't practical (E. Ambry, personal communication, February 10, 2002).

> When I was hired as a full-time person [at the New Jersey State School of Conservation], I worked with the six [New Jersey] State Teacher Colleges, and one of the responsibilities was to winterize the . . . camp so it could be used year-round. They set up a requirement for every sophomore from the six colleges . . . to go to camp for one week as part of their student teaching program. . . . Two colleges decided to [send students] in their junior year where it would tie in more with their other student teaching blocks for courses. That was Trenton and Paterson, I think. The others, they all went on

their sophomore year (C. Emanuelson, personal communication, January 21, 2002).

Unfinished Book Projects

Many photographs of L. B. Sharp and Life Camps were taken over the years by Donald Rettew, a National Camp staff member and later a professional photographer in Merion, Pennsylvania. Sharp, in writing to Rettew in 1959, told of the heavy workload he was carrying in completing several survey reports and architectural designs. He was behind in completing these endeavors and felt "very much pressured" (Sharp, 1959a, p. 1). This letter was a response to previous letters and discussions with Rettew where both men had expressed concern over the work of the Outdoor Education Association primarily being carried on by Sharp himself. Sharp explained to Rettew that there was no time to make long-range plans or to try to enlist help from others. Furthermore, the funds for the Outdoor Education Association were about depleted. He wrote,

> If I do not do these [surveys] regardless of anything else we will have nothing to do anything with. So far, I have been able to break even and that is all. My NYU earnings last year will cover me for almost two years, last and this, but will not quite make it (Sharp, 1959a, p. 1).

Located in the same envelope with Sharp's (1959a) letter and other correspondence with Don Rettew was an outline of photo book ideas that had apparently been previously discussed between Sharp and Rettew. One of Rettew's proposed ideas was that a small photo book titled This is Camping should be published containing his own photographs of Life Camps. The book would be marketed with the strategic intent of bringing needed publicity to the Outdoor Education Association and National Camp. Another idea on Rettew's list was a proposed book called Moccasins. He included this quote in his description, "You can tell where the lamplighter has been by the trail of light he has left behind" (Rettew, 1959, p. 1). Sharp's response to Rettew was that photo books would be too expensive to produce, sales would be doubtful and that he could not handle any more projects or new plans at that time. However, he also wrote that a book of photos of the handmade camping shelters might work (Sharp, 1959a).

After Sharp's death, Luther Lindenmuth (1964), a National Camp and Life Camp staff member and previous director of the NJSSC, also described a book project he had worked on at one time with Sharp, seemingly the same Moccasins book discussed above by Rettew. Lindenmuth wrote, "In 1958, one of our projects was to start on his book, Moccasin Trails, wherein he was to publish his stories and adventures. . . . As far as I know nothing more was ever done. He was too busy doing the things he enjoyed and had to do to further the movement" (p. 1).

Don Hammerman recalled a personal conversation with Sharp pertaining to the same book project, and gave this account:

> The other thing I recall about one of L. B.'s visits was he was telling me that he had never written a book. He wanted to write one someday. All of his writings, for the most part, were articles or the talks he gave. If he wrote a book, he said . . . each chapter would be based on his moccasins. He told me how many moccasins he had worn out in his life. It might have been 22 pairs of moccasins. The first chapter would be the first pair of moccasins and what transpired in his life during that first pair of moccasins, and the second pair, and the third pair, and so on. And I thought, well, that's kind of a neat idea, but he never got around to doing it (D. Hammerman, personal communication, January 6, 2002).

In the Sharp Papers collection at the Morris Library at Southern Illinois University, several undated outlines and notes written in Sharp's handwriting reveal that he had a collection of book ideas throughout his career. The title of one of his book ideas was *Outdoor Education and Camping Education*. He had outlined and titled nine chapters for this book. The names of other books Sharp planned to write included *Real Camps* or *Real Camping, My Tepee, A New Grip in Learning: School Camps and Outdoor Education*, and *A Certain Kansas Lad*. He also had listed plans for a book on the American Chestnut tree, travel trailer camping, and shelters (The L. B. Sharp Papers, 2002).

Ed Ambry revealed that he has a transcript of one of Sharp's books in his possession. He explained,

> L. B. Sharp's secretary sat and let L. B. Sharp dictate to her something that was called *The Kansas Lad* . . . I can't really put a date on it, but it was when he was at Southern Illinois. . . . It was dictated to his secretary and sent to me. I did share that with several people. It's about a 20-page document that he felt, in his later years, that he should tell to someone. . . . It's almost a complete history of his life (E. Ambry, personal communication, February 10, 2002).

It appears that *A Certain Kansas Lad* may have been the only book authored by Sharp that was completed. However, according to Ambry, it is doubtful that the book was ever advanced in the publishing process beyond the transcription.

Lecturer at New York University

For the 1957–58 academic year, Sharp renewed his relationship with NYU to some extent by securing a position with the title of lecturer in education, teaching on a part-time basis (Sharp, 1957). At this point, Sharp was 62 years of age. He was filling in for another professor who would be away on a sabbatical leave during that academic year. Bob Christie described his contact with Sharp during that time through the following explanation:

> I was teaching at Scarsdale, New York, which was 20 miles outside New York City . . . and L. B. was at New York University. I . . . went down to help him with some of his courses. . . . He was on the faculty at NYU. We remained in contact there. I moved into classroom teaching, because I felt I needed to

have the classroom teaching experience. I was a physical education teacher at Scarsdale. I couldn't understand why classroom teachers weren't picking up on the outdoor education, so I became a classroom teacher so I could do that. I was in contact with L. B. at that time (R. Christie, personal communication, May 9, 2002).

— 5 —

Relocation to Southern Illinois University (1959–1963)

In 1952 Sharp had been hired to conduct a land survey by Delyte Morris, the eighth president of Southern Illinois University (SIU) at Carbondale, Illinois. Morris was known to carry in his pocket a small folded piece of paper on which he had handwritten his ten-year plan for the university for the years 1952 to 1962. The list contained plans for the development of an outdoor public school facility on property owned by the university on the shores of Little Grassy Lake within a short drive of the campus (Mitchell, 1988).

The university owned 200 acres of forested land and leased 150 more acres a few miles south of Carbondale. Morris was interested in developing an outdoor education center for use by the university students and the kindergarten through twelfth grade children who attended the University School operated by SIU. Across the lake from the SIU property were an additional 1,400 acres owned by the Federal Fish and Wildlife Service (FFWS). The 1,400 acres were leased by a group formed in 1949 known as the Educational Council of 100 and made up of educators and citizens from 31 southern Illinois counties (Sharp, 1961a). Morris planned to work cooperatively with the FFWS and the Educational Council of 100 to create the outdoor education center. Sharp was hired to survey the properties, design facilities, and develop a plan for such an endeavor (Sharp, 1952).

Invitation from President Morris

During the years following Sharp's initial survey report, the acreage owned by SIU was developed and used by the university for students and other groups. However, the plans for the property owned by the FFWS had not yet been realized at the time Morris approached Sharp about coming to work at SIU in the late 1950s. Morris invited Sharp to continue the implementation of the SIU outdoor education plan as a university faculty member. Sharp spent time seriously considering Morris' offer due to circumstances in the east that were increasingly making it unfavorable for him to stay there. Narrators described the events leading up to Sharp's move to Southern Illinois University in their own following words:

> [By the late 1950s], Bill Palmer . . . began to cool off a little on his support of the property [at Pole Bridge] even though L. B. Sharp struggled like mad doing these camp surveys and giving these talks. The camp surveys were actually bringing money into the Outdoor Education Association (T. Rillo, personal communication, December 27, 2001).

> L. B. . . . . fell on some hard times in New York. His Outdoor Education Association, Incorporated, wasn't doing well financially, as I recall. It was losing membership and that kind of thing. There was a conference at Bradford Woods. . . . L. B. was not there, but Julian Smith, Rey Carlson, and some of the other people from SIU [were there]. One of the questions that was discussed was, 'What are we going to do about L. B.?' The guy was almost down and out. What [could] be done to give him a boost and keep his association going? One of the suggestions was that some institution ought to offer him a visiting professorship, and SIU did capitalize on that. He wound up there for the remainder of his career (D. Hammerman, personal communication, January 6, 2002).

I think the opportunity to teach at SIU appealed to him because of President Delyte Morris, who was a visionary and had
accumulated over 2,000 acres of land. The idea that he would
have a lot of freedom to develop a program of outdoor education on all this land and the support of the university president was very appealing. I doubt if he got that support at NYU
(C. Knapp, personal communication, December 19, 2001).

Somewhat secretively, Sharp accepted Morris' offer to move to
Carbondale. Sharp wrote to an associate, Bill Goodall, to inform
him that he was already at SIU and working in a position as a visiting professor for one academic year, that of 1959–1960 (Sharp,
1959b). Narrator Ed Ambry described Sharp's new position:

When L. B. Sharp left New York City, he went to Southern Illinois as a visiting professor. He was able to do a lot of things
because he only taught a course once in a while. . . . The university was very generous with him. He knew the president
very well. They offered him space [for the OEA] at no charge,
and use of automobiles and other things that college professors and administrators have (E. Ambry, personal communication, February 10, 2002).

During the summer of 1960, arrangements were finalized for
Sharp to continue employment at SIU under the title of profes-
sor-lecturer of Outdoor Education. His appointment there was to
be continuous, yet renewed on a yearly basis. His assignment was
as an interdepartmental faculty member and also as a staff member for the Little Grassy Lake Campus. He was to be hired on a
half-time basis of $6,000 annually. Sharp's appointment was ar-
ranged as a halftime position in order to allow him to continue the
promotional work of the OEA, which included speaking engage-
ments, consultant work, and design surveys. In writing to William
Freeberg, chair of the Recreation Department at the time, Sharp
(1960b) indicated that talks of permanently moving the OEA to
SIU were being considered. To do so, however, he explained that a

more stable, long-range plan concerning his annual contract would be necessary.

Associates of Sharp were apparently under the impression that his position at SIU was stable since earlier, in the spring of 1960, some of them began to make arrangements to attend SIU (Ambry, 1960). Edward Ambry, OEA board member and faculty member at Montclair State College in New Jersey at the time, arranged to take a leave of absence from Montclair to work on doctoral studies under Sharp. He added the following comments regarding his move to SIU:

> I was working on my doctor's degree at New York University and L. B. Sharp was on my committee [when he went to SIU] . . . so, I took a year's leave of absence . . . and went out to Carbondale. I taught half-time . . . and got my residency. . . . He was still on my committee, but he passed away before either Tom Rillo or I . . . were finished (E. Ambry, personal communication, February 10, 2002).

Tom Rillo, also a faculty member at Montclair, also made leave arrangements to attend SIU to pursue his doctorate. He expounded,

> I had followed [L. B.] to SIU in 1960 to do my doctorate. He was going to be [the] chair of my doctoral study. Ed Ambry and I had gone out there together and we had visited with L. B. By that time, the university had given him the bid. . . . So now [I was] at Southern Illinois University . . . working for L. B. Sharp as a graduate assistant doing camp surveys primarily and going to class and teaching. That was a great time . . . (T. Rillo, personal communication, December 27, 2001).

Two years later, Clifford Knapp, a former staff member at NJSCC, also enrolled in graduate school at SIU to work under Sharp. He explained,

> [I] went to Carbondale, Illinois, to study under L. B. Sharp at the university. There, I got a graduate teaching assistantship, assigned to L. B. I would take him and pick him up at the

airport when he went on his trips to do master planning or to speak at different conferences. So, I had a chance to ride in the car back and forth from these frequent trips. He was earning what I thought was a phenomenal consultant fee of $100 a day. I was in awe of that (C. Knapp, personal communication, December 19, 2001).

I spent that year getting my master's degree in educational administration and supervision and studying under him and doing whatever he needed me to do. I conducted some workshop sessions and went with him to some of the conferences where he spoke. He taught me how to color a master plan map that he presented to each organization that he worked for (C. Knapp, personal communication, December 19, 2001).

Sharp must have, at some point, felt secure enough with his SIU arrangement to officially move the OEA headquarters to Carbondale during the fall of 1960. The creation of a national reference library on outdoor education was part of the negotiations in moving the headquarters. The plan was for the OEA to turn over its extensive collection of books, research studies, and other documents to this new national library, which would be housed by SIU's Morris Library (Sharp, 1961b).

A year after the OEA records were relocated to SIU, Sharp sent letters to Russ and Helena Rayner, the directors at Pole Bridge Camp, informing them that Pole Bridge and National Camp were to be immediately dismantled and moved by freight car to the Little Grassy Lake Campus (Sharp, 1961b). This letter was followed a few days later with similar letters to former staff members (Sharp, 1961c) and campers (Sharp, 1961d). The move was explained by Sharp as necessary, partly due to recurring financial deficits for Pole Bridge Camp. There was also a desire to make alternative arrangements for the use of the camp by William E. Palmer, the owner of the property.

In discussing the plans to relocate Pole Bridge Camp, Sharp (1961b) referred to the early years at Life Camps from 1926 to 1928 and beyond as the time when the "small group process in camping" (p. 1) was developed. He described the years of 1925 to 1940 as "an era of study, experimentation, and evaluation" (p. 1). He further explained, "We have come to a point of redirection though basic aims and purposes will change very little" (p. 1). Sharp explained in his letter to the Rayners,

> You may be sure it is and will be difficult for me and others to leave the 'Heart of the Hills,' a land we did not have to learn to love. We came to it and it loved us. The roots there placed were alive, tender, and deep. With these roots gently removed, in part, is a plan to replant them in other areas (p. 1).

According to a news release from SIU, the relocation of the camps involved transporting 15 tons of equipment. Some of the items identified included covered "Conestoga" wagons, tepees, shelters, and library materials (Lyons, 1961). Ed Ambry recalled,

> We even took covered wagons out there. We dismantled them and put them in trucks. We used to kid about it. In early America, everybody went across the country in covered wagons, and these were the last covered wagons to go west from New York (E. Ambry, personal communication, February 10, 2002).

New Plans and Uncertainty for Little Grassy Lake Campus

Sharp conducted a 1961 revision of the original 1952 development plan for the Little Grassy property. The revision included plans for a center for advanced leadership preparation in outdoor education, as well as the originally planned residential center for public schools in the southern Illinois area. The residential center was to be developed on the 1,400 acres owned in 1952 by the U. S. Fish and Wildlife Service across the lake from the other camps that had been developed at the Little Grassy Lake Campus (Sharp, 1961a).

Cliff Knapp's description of Sharp's first attempt at relocating the Pole Bridge Camp structures explains:

> When I first went out there [to SIU] in the summer of '62, I was on [L. B.'s] camp staff. There were only about eight campers and that was the replication of his Pole Bridge Camp decentralized model. That was on the west side of Little Grassy Lake where the old camps had been established for years. We were just one cell within what they called Camp 1 then. . . . That was his only attempt at establishing a camp for kids in the midwest because it never happened after that. I don't think it happened in the summer of '63. So I had the privilege of working as one of the staff in his last children's camps. I've got that pretty well recorded because I used the experience in the first course I took with him. It was an independent study in which my task was to record the story of this camp (C. Knapp, personal communication, December 19, 2001).

By December of 1962, it appeared that plans for a national leadership site and development of the residential outdoor center for schools, now called the SIBOGI project, were not progressing as anticipated. Members of the OEA Steering Committee constructed a letter to Sharp, with his approval, for use in spurring SIU to move forward with the plans. The letter was from Matthew J. Brennan, chairman of the Steering Committee. The letter requested that Sharp make a report at an upcoming OEA Board of Directors' meeting in Atlantic City. The report should inform the board of the current status of the cooperative arrangement between SIU and OEA and of the plans to develop SIBOGI, National Camp, and a national center for outdoor education at SIU. The letter further requested information on the intended development of the outdoor education library that was to be maintained as part of the Morris Library at SIU (Brennan, 1962).

Sharp responded to Brennan's letter with words of gratitude for the letter which could be used "here at the University for a crowbar" (Sharp, 1962, p. 1). Sharp had met with John E. Grinnell, the vice-president of SIU, and told him that it "would be very embarrassing and probably hurtful for SIU if I had to report no progress" (p. 2). The concerns of the OEA Steering Committee were reiterated in a status report sent to Sharp after the Atlantic City Board of Directors' meeting in February of 1963. The report mentioned the "uncertainty of the future relationship between Southern Illinois University and the Outdoor Education Association" (Brennan, 1963, p. 1). Regarding the situation, Clifford Knapp surmised,

> [L. B.] was just one person. He had a secretary and one graduate assistant probably. I was his only assistant that year, but I think he might have had one or two the next year. And if he got a lot of master plans or a lot of speeches which took him away, then he couldn't do other work. I would not be surprised that the Association suffered (C. Knapp, personal communication, December 19, 2001).

There were apparently some personnel moves occurring at the Little Grassy Lake Campus during the spring of 1963. Sharp (1963c) wrote to Ambry and Rillo, who had finished their doctoral coursework and returned to work at Montclair State College while finishing their dissertations. He stated, "I'm being pressed now to make a start with the SIBOGI project. It is too involved to explain. I am starting all over. They want to send out some chipped up barracks. I am preparing a plan to implement the Outdoor Education Center master plan" (p. 1). This same letter announced that Loren Taylor, an SIU faculty member and director of the Little Grassy Lake Campus, had been moved from directing Little Grassy and would be helping Sharp 25 percent of the time.

A letter written from Loren Taylor (1963) to Donald Hammerman, then the assistant director of Lorado Taft Field Campus, confirmed that he had been assigned back to the main campus and was primarily teaching. He also wrote that Bill Price had been hired to replace him as the new director of Little Grassy, the future plans for which would be group use, conferences, and recreational activities. Taylor informed Hammerman that outdoor education would be emphasized through Sharp's projects across the lake. Ed Ambry's comment on these moves posited:

> There was a power struggle . . . that might not have affected L. B. too much because he was actually trying to develop something across the lake from the Little Grassy site (E. Ambry, personal communication, February 10, 2002).

Around this time in 1963, yet another former National Camp staff member was making plans for graduate studies under Sharp at SIU and offered the following explanation:

> I needed a Ph.D., so I made arrangements and talked with L. B. about coming out as a graduate assistant and working with him and doing my Ph.D. at Southern Illinois University. Unfortunately, I initiated the application work in the fall and that year, 1963, Kennedy was assassinated. A day or two days later, my father died. And then I think it was either two or three weeks later, L. B. died. That was not a good year, but I continued and moved to SIU. Tom Rillo came [back from Montclair] to SIU to replace L. B. . . . I did my Ph.D. under Tom, but I was going there because L. B. was there and I had done all the initial work with L. B. (R. Christie, personal communication, May 9, 2002).

Sharp had been developing his plans for the new outdoor education center into a display named "Land for Learning" to be presented at the American Association of School Administrators Convention in Atlantic City in February 1964. The display was forty feet long and seven feet high, featuring enlarged photographs of sites from the property on Little Grassy Lake (Brinley, 1964).

Sharp (1963d) crafted a letter to C. D. Jackson, the publisher of *Life* magazine in New York. Sharp indicated that he and Jackson had not had any contact since Life Camps were dissolved and National Camp moved to the Pole Bridge Camp site in the early 1950s. He wrote to inform Jackson of the upcoming "Land for Learning" exhibit at the Atlantic City convention that usually attracted more than 25,000 school administrators. The enormous exhibit would introduce the new outdoor education center being developed on the east side of Little Grassy Lake on 2,000 acres of old farmland. Sharp inquired as to whether *Life* magazine would be willing to publish a feature presentation on "Land for Learning" the week before the convention.

The plans for the outdoor education center at SIU included the residential elementary program for use by the 31 counties in southern Illinois, day programs using resource-filled trailers for secondary students, college courses for teachers, and master's and doctoral students in education. Outdoor leadership preparation institutes such as those conducted at National Camp and other related projects would also be implemented. A usage rate of over 37,000 students per year had been estimated by Sharp (*Land for Learning*, 1964).

The Outdoor Education Center, now written with capital letters, received its first students during October of 1963. An elementary school from Perry County, Illinois, and a junior high school from Cutler, Illinois, brought the first groups to attend. The program was described as being sponsored by SIU, OEA, and the Educational Council of 100 ("Outdoor Education Center opens today at Little Grassy," 1963).

Don Hammerman recounted one of Sharp's final pieces of writing, which was completed within a month of the first group's attendance at the Outdoor Education Center:

> L. B. wrote the 'Foreword' to the first and second edition of *Teaching in the Outdoors* [by Hammerman, Hammerman and Hammerman, 1964; 1973]. The first edition was dedicated to him. . . . I think he wrote it in November, as I recall. . . . He must have written it shortly before he died (D. Hammerman, personal communication, January 6, 2002).

— 6 —

The Passing of Lloyd Burgess Sharp (1963 and Beyond)

On December 5, 1963, a telegram was sent from Western Union at noon to a dozen close associates of Sharp from his secretary, Connie Beckett. The message announced, "Father of Outdoor Education has passed away. December 4 on a field trip in Florida. Dr. Sharp suffered fatal heart attack. Expect programs to continue. Funeral arrangements handled Topeka, Kansas" (Beckett, 1963, no page). Soon afterward, Ann Brinley, chair of the OEA membership committee, and Edward Ambry, secretary-treasurer, sent out the following announcement:

> All who have been associated with L. B. Sharp will want to know of his untimely death December 4, 1963, while on a field survey in Florida. For him, it was the way he would choose to go, doing the work he loved best (Brinley & Ambry, 1963, p. 1).

Information was provided in the announcement that Sharp had already prepared the OEA annual Christmas greeting card for that year. The OEA intended to follow through on mailing the card, especially since it featured a photograph of Sharp next to his tepee overlooking the view from the knoll at Pole Bridge Camp, and a poem that he had written about the area. The poem was entitled "Heart-of-the-Hills View" (see Appendix B).

Sharp spent his last few days with Reverend Warren W. Willis, with whom he traveled from southern to northern Florida to survey two properties and create master plans for a Methodist church camp at each site. Willis (1963) immediately wrote to Sharp's only child, Frances Barkmann of Sante Fe, New Mexico, to inform her of the last few days of Sharp's life. He described Sharp as being in "good spirits and his usual jovial mood all day" (p. 1).

Willis (1963) explained that he and Sharp had arrived at Mayo, Florida, and checked into a motel around 7:00 p.m. on December 4, 1963. The two men ate dinner together and retired to their rooms. Sharp told Willis he planned to finish some notes for the survey work. Around 9:15 p.m., the local sheriff arrived at Willis' room and informed him that Sharp had died of an apparent heart attack about three blocks away from the motel. Willis wrote, "those who saw him said he just clutched his stomach or chest and fell over, one man catching him and easing him down. It was sudden and quick" (p. 1).

Willis' (1963) letter also informed Sharp's daughter that during their last days together, L. B. had talked several times of her and his grandchildren, as well as other children he loved. Willis told of a conversation where Sharp said he felt "God as a part of himself that he could not lose even if he wanted to" (p. 1).

The narrators vividly recalled hearing the news of Sharp's death and provided the following recollections:

> Ed Ambry gave me a call. I was up here in Connecticut at the time. I went out to Kansas for the funeral. . . . Fortunately, he went quick when he went. He was on the job down in Florida and walking along the street and just fell over and that was it. That's the way I want to go (C. Emanuelson, personal communication, January 21, 2002).

When L. B. Sharp died, I happened to be at a conference somewhere. Instead of coming home, I got on a plane and went to his funeral (E. Ambry, personal communication, February 10, 2002).

That's a kind of a funny thing, a saying that L. B. Sharp had. He was born in Carbondale, Kansas, and he died in Carbondale, Illinois. He used to always have some fun saying, 'I never got very far from Carbondale to Carbondale' (E. Ambry, personal communication, February 10, 2002).

A few days after his death, friends and associates received cards and letters Sharp had mailed to them. The time and date on the postmarks of these letters indicate that Sharp had mailed them just previous to his death (Brinley, 1964). A letter from Sharp to Loren Taylor said that he was in Mayo, Florida, and would see Taylor on the next Saturday (Taylor, n.d.).

Sharp's funeral service was held outdoors in Carbondale, Kansas, where he was buried in the local Carbondale Cemetery ("Lloyd B. Sharp ex-Carbondale doctor is dead," 1963) near the gravesites of his parents and his two older brothers who had preceded him in death. A rough draft of the OEA newsletter being compiled for January 1964 read that greenery, cones, and chestnut bundles had been collected by Donald Rettew and William Palmer from the knoll at Pole Bridge Camp site and displayed at the funeral (Brinley, 1964).

Sharp had been close to his niece, Jean Sticher, of Topeka, Kansas. After the funeral, she received a letter from Luther Lindenmuth (1964), who had been a National Camp and Life Camp staff member, describing his memories of Sharp. Lindenmuth wrote that he had been at Sharp's 2,000th tepee fire celebration.

Continuing the Journey

After Sharp's death, the OEA board members met and appointed DeAlton Partridge, president of Montclair State College in New Jersey, as the new OEA president. Thomas Rillo had been recruited from Montclair State College to continue Sharp's work as coordinator of the Outdoor Education Center at SIU (Brinley, 1964).

Some of the narrators who were involved in continuing Sharp's work after his death described their perspective of the situation in the following segments:

> We operated [the OEA] when L. B. Sharp died. We pulled together with a couple of people, sort of a self-appointed group to carry on the work, but this group, like myself, were employed doing something else . . . a kind of an 'ad hoc' organization without any money. When L. B. Sharp died, in his budget there was only about $10,000 or less. I became the treasurer and tried to raise money from different places, and we did for a while. [Eventually] it just kind of withered on the vine (E. Ambry, personal communication, February 10, 2002).

> I [was] nearing the end of my [doctoral] coursework, and L. B. Sharp pass[ed] away doing a camp survey in Mayo, Florida. . . . I was called back by Bill Freeberg to carry on L. B.'s work. I had gone back to Montclair State where I was an assistant professor. I [became] the main coordinator of the Outdoor Education Center. . . . The forty southernmost counties of southern Illinois were coming together in a consortium. The trailers would ply their way into these communities. Each trailer would have two graduate students. They would do workshops. We did this for a while, Cliff [Knapp] and I, Bob Christie, Fred Korach, Butch Christie. . . . Across the lake, we had the Daisy Farm. The university had picked up this farm. It was at this farm that L. B. Sharp had devised his master plan for outdoor education with schools, and we implemented that. I became coordinator of that as well as an associate professor. So I taught courses out there. I also taught courses on campus (T. Rillo, personal communication, December 27, 2001).

> After [obtaining my master's degree at SIU], I went to New York City to teach . . . in the Riverdale section of the Bronx, and then one day a week I would take the subway down to mid-town Manhattan and teach science at their other school. Central Park was my outdoor laboratory. I was only there one

year because that was the year that L. B. Sharp passed away in December 1963. The following year in '64, Tom Rillo replaced L. B. and I was brought in as the assistant coordinator for the Outdoor Education Center at Southern Illinois. . . . We were trying to carry on what L. B. had started (C. Knapp, personal communication, December 19, 2001).

There were a number of OEA business concerns that needed attention. In the late spring of 1964, arrangements were made for some of the OEA officers and secretary to attempt to complete work on the surveys and master plans that Sharp had not yet finished when he died. Ed Ambry recalled,

> When he died, there were 21 of those [master plans] that were not finished. Ann Brinley and I finished all 21. I know we didn't do as well as Sharp would have done, but we tried to finish the contracts on them. . . . Sometimes, we never got paid because it wasn't L. B. Sharp's work, but we put it together. We were just trying to be honest and finish things up. We didn't care about the money (E. Ambry, personal communication, February 10, 2002).

After Sharp's death, John Grinnell, vice-president of SIU, recommended to Delyte Morris that the Outdoor Education Center under construction at Little Grassy Lake be named the "L. B. Sharp Outdoor Education Center" (Ambry, 1964). The name proposed by Grinnell was not adopted. The properties on both the west and east side of Little Grassy Lake were named the "Outdoor Laboratories," a name still in use in 1972. Some years later, yet another name was given, that of the "Touch of Nature Environmental Center," the name that is still in use today (Southern Illinois University, 2002).

In May of 1964, a fund drive was launched by the Educational Council of 100 to raise $250,000 to develop the Little Grassy Lake area. A newspaper account reported that the money would be used to develop 900 acres owned by SIU and 1,800 acres leased from the U.S. Fish and Wildlife Service. The funds would be enough to pay for half the cost of building a dining hall, administration building, library, health building, sleeping quarters, and restoration of an old farm. SIU planned on contributing another $193,000 for roads, a sewage treatment plant, parking, and service buildings ("Area fund drive planned for wilderness classroom," 1964). The article did not indicate from what source the other half of the building funds would be provided. More changes occurred a few years later and were described as,

> Tom Rillo left SIU after three or four years and went to Glassboro State College in New Jersey. Then, [SIU] brought in a new director. I didn't have my doctorate at that point. . . . For a period of maybe nine months to a year, I was acting coordinator until they brought in a fellow named Paul Nowak. I became Paul Nowak's assistant for the remainder of my time there. Then I went to Ridgewood, New Jersey, where I was the outdoor education and science specialist for the whole district. . . . I left there in December 1979. . . . [There was] an opening for the director of Lorado Taft Field Campus. It seemed to be just the right thing for me. . . . So, I handwrote an application. . . . In those days, it was a combined position—director of Lorado Taft Field Campus and chair of the outdoor education faculty, and I got it (C. Knapp, personal communication, December 19, 2001).

Memorial Library at the New Jersey State School of Conservation

In May of 1964, the New Jersey State School of Conservation dedicated its library to Sharp and renamed it the L. B. Sharp Memorial Library. A dedication ceremony was held on May 6. Lawrence H. Conrad, professor emeritus at Montclair State College in New Jersey, presented a tribute to Sharp that was later published in 1972 in *Perspectives on Outdoor Education: Readings* by Donaldson and Goering. In Conrad's (1964) memorial dedication, he said that Sharp, put his career and his life as it turned out, into one vital and potent idea, and he lived to see some phases of that idea pervade the whole structure of the American educational system. If he was disappointed in not seeing his entire program adopted in his lifetime, this is a disappointment not uncommon to those who see farther than the rest of us (p. 1–2).

The L. B. Sharp Memorial Library still exists at the NJSSC and displays some of the original photographs of L. B. taken by photographer and National Camper Donald Rettew.

Memorial Conference

On October 1, 2, and 3 of 1965, the L. B. Sharp Memorial Outdoor Education Conference was sponsored by the New Jersey Outdoor Education Association and the National Outdoor Education Association. The conference was based at the New Jersey State School of Conservation, but included day trips to the nearby Pinchot Institute and the original National Camp site near Sussex, New Jersey. The conference offered an assortment of familiar National Camp activities such as "bull sessions," "stump scouting," orienteering, square dancing, and a culminating "buffalo throw." Discussions and keynote sessions were also organized that addressed the future outlook for outdoor education (New Jersey Outdoor Education Association and the National Outdoor Education Association, 1965).

A memorial service for Sharp was held the first night of the conference and led by Reverend Maurice D. Bone, who had worked closely with Sharp on church camp leadership endeavors. Memorial tributes to Sharp were given throughout the weekend by his friends and associates. One of these was a poem written by Millard van Dien (1965), former Life Camp staff member, and read by Ginger Emanuelson, the wife of Cliff Emanuelson, one of the narrators for this study. (See Appendix C.)

Memorial Library at Southern Illinois University

Years later at SIU, while still named the Outdoor Laboratories, another library was dedicated to Sharp at the Little Grassy Lake site. Paul Yambert had become the dean of the Outdoor Laboratories in 1969, as well as an SIU faculty member, and was instrumental in establishing a memorial library dedicated to Sharp. With the help and support of Edward Ambry, Ann Brinley, and the Outdoor Education Association, Yambert organized Sharp's private collection of books and documents, his personal artifacts, and OEA materials that were still located at the Little Grassy site. He provided the following perspective on his preparation of the memorial library there:

> There were three or four people, including Ed Ambry, [who] all touched base and agreed that this was an idea [for which] its time had probably come. . . . [P]artly because of self-serving interests that we thought this might make more people aware of the fact that there was this place called Little Grassy. But also, that there was too much that Sharp had done to just let it disintegrate (P. Yambert, personal communication, March 24, 2002).

> We had all these little things like the chestnut wood and the Bowie knives and the arrowheads he collected and the fossils he collected and all this kind of stuff. He had a weird collection of stuff. So we envisioned a library where there would be rotating display cases of some of his possessions and some of his writings and maybe a few of his hand-painted master plans for camps—things that he and his graduate students had done. . . . So, basically, we took a building and made it into a fairly attractive building and started to try to move in the books and get them organized and then move in the other stuff. . . . If I had to give credit to one person, it would be Ann Brinley. . . . As I recall, she came at least two summers, maybe more, and worked just dawn to dusk on this trying to make things fall into place. She had a lot of the background information on what L. B. was trying to do. [There was L. B.'s] willow bed that she had kept the wands for if some of them

The
L. B. Sharp Memorial

Outdoor Education Conference

"That which can best be learned in the Classroom

should be learned there . . .

. . . that which can best be learned in the out-of-doors,

through direct experience,

dealing with native materials and real life situations,

should be learned there."

L. B. SHARP

October 1, 2 & 3, 1965

The Pinchot Institute for Studies in Conservation, Milford, Pennsylvania
N.J. State School of Conservation, Stokes Forest, Branchville, N.J.
National Camp, Lake Mishipacong, High Point St. Park, N.J.

would get broken. . . . There was also about . . . four four-drawer file cabinets that . . . had a hodge-podge of things from petty cash to uncashed checks that L. B. had used as bookmarks. I had heard about those, and it's actually true. They were definitely in there. . . . There was a mixture of old master plans for camps. . . . They did some beautiful water-color paintings of these things, just like an architect would do for a home (P. Yambert, personal communication, March 24, 2002).

A lamp and desk made of American chestnut, handmade by Millard van Dien, and chestnut bookshelves and tables were to be kept at the library also (Ambry & Yambert, 1972).

The dedication ceremony for the L. B. Sharp Memorial Library and Resource Center was held May 6, 1972. A "buffalo throw" was held, as well as a tour of the facilities, then described as entailing 7,000 acres of land. Exhibits planned for the library were described in the registration brochure as "L. B. the camper, innovator, paint-er, poet, photographer, story-teller, master-planner, educator, and above all, friend to all" (Ambry & Yambert, 1972, p. 1). Small memorial chestnut wood bundles were passed out at the dedication ceremony. Yambert further described preparing the bundles:

> I found a wicker basket with these little pieces of wood, prob-ably a foot to a foot and a half long. Being a forester, I rec-ognized them as chestnut. . . . So, what I did was split them using one of L. B. Sharp's knives. He left several Bowie knives around. . . . We found a piece of his personally tanned deer-hide and cut it into strips and used it to wrap. We put the bookmark from the new library around the bundle originally and then tied that with the leather thong (P. Yambert, per-sonal communication, March 24, 2002).

In discussing whatever happened to the development of the SIBOGI project and the farmland on the east side of Little Grassy Lake, Yambert explained that new construction across the lake had been limited to a single large log cabin structure with a rock fireplace. During his time there, arsonists burned down the structure, destroying artifacts in the process. Delyte Morris and Yambert discussed rebuilding and concluded that the Outdoor Education Center and Little Grassy should be merged. Camp Oikos, a Greek word meaning *ecology*, was created as an ecologically sound residential outdoor education area back on the west side of the lake (P. Yambert, personal communication, March 24, 2002). Eventually, in 1970, Delyte Morris retired or was removed from office due to health concerns (Mitchell, 1988), and any future plans for expansion of outdoor education dissolved. Yambert was reassigned away from the Little Grassy site to the main SIU campus a few years later and recounted,

> When I left . . . with Delyte gone, it was clear that the vice-president was going to take over and didn't want to spend this money on Little Grassy. . . . I didn't have any choice, but it was a mutual understanding that I was not interested in going into the business of running a camp. They were not interested in having an academician out there who just wanted to spend money on programs. So, I just went back to the campus and did my thing for the next 18 years (P. Yambert, personal communication, March 24, 2002).

> One of the last things I did before leaving Little Grassy was load up a truck and put those four cabinets of files of L. B.'s on that. . . . I had a pretty good working relationship with the librarian on the campus because we had talked about making the L. B. Library an official sub-unit of the campus library. So, I had explained to him that those books were probably going to get burned or something. We hauled up everything I could get my hands on while we still had the authority to do it and took them up. The good news was that that provided a place where they were relatively safe. The bad news was that the library had other higher priorities. So for several years, the stuff just basically sat there as far as I know (P. Yambert, personal communication, March 24, 2002).

At that point, the [outdoor education] center idea sort of went up in smoke with the cabin. Instead of that, we saw Little Grassy in its entirety as the outdoor education center. So the whole thing then was renamed Touch of Nature. . . . To me, there is irony in the name. Delyte and I wanted more than 'a touch' of nature (P. Yambert, personal communication, March 24, 2002).

Recollections of L. B. Sharp

The following narrative segments are general statements made by the narrators about Sharp. Some of these segments describe memories that made special impressions. Some of them summarize Sharp's life, career, or accomplishments.

> I think he was very disappointed in the end. I think he was very happy doing what he was doing. . . . When he died, he was doing exactly what he did all his life. . . . The fact that he didn't have enough energy and enough to keep going, I don't think he felt sorry for himself at all, but he was disappointed. . . . I think he felt that he didn't do enough. I guess all of us, when we're getting ready to die, think that we never really reached what we wanted to do (E. Ambry, personal communication, February 10, 2002).

> [Being at SIU with L. B.] was a great time, except that I don't think L. B. Sharp was completely happy. I think it was sort of a let down. . . . He didn't achieve his vision of seeing schools embrace outdoor education and training teachers at the level and scale and numbers that he wanted to see. He felt that this was nipping the bud and perhaps if things had been different maybe he could reach more teachers, more superintendents. In fact, he began to do workshops for administrators in that decade between 1950 and 1960. He began to do administrative workshops because he knew that the answer lay with the administrator. If the administrator said, 'Yes, we're going to have outdoor education,' you're going to have outdoor

education (T. Rillo, personal communication, December 27, 2001).

As L. B. said, 'It takes years and years and years of experience.' I don't know how many times I heard him say that (R. Christie, personal communication, May 9, 2002).

L. B. was a good buddy. . . . When we were together, we'd enjoy one another's company (D. Hammerman, personal communication, January 6, 2002).

My wife and I lived in his apartment . . . about two weeks before my daughter, Dawn, was born so that we would be in town closer to the hospital. We were living at Little Grassy Lake right before the birth date. My daughter was born November 22, 1963. I have a photo of L. B. holding my daughter. . . . He would come to visit my wife and I and our small baby, Dawn . . . and bring an aluminum coffee pot of whiskey sours. We would sit around and talk. . . . Probably that didn't happen more than two or three times, but for me it's so clear I thought maybe it happened more often, but it didn't. I can remember writing something right after he had returned home and thinking about the significance of that meeting with him. I was in awe of him, naturally. It was really a family kind of feeling that I had. I was a thousand miles from my parents in New Jersey, and didn't have any family there, so he became a pseudo-father, and mentor, and teacher, and boss (C. Knapp, personal communication, December 19, 2001).

L. B. Sharp used to wonder why people admired him so. I remember in one conversation—I remember it only because I wrote it down—he was wondering why people admired him so. He wasn't an expert in any one thing. He was a generalist. I know why people admired him, but he wasn't quite sure why people did (C. Knapp, personal communication, December 19, 2001).

The nature of my relationship with Dr. Sharp was as an inspirational teacher, motivational leader, resourceful pioneer and informative mentor in the field of camping, and outdoor education. . . . His legacy has been lasting . . . a treasure of life (E. Morrison, personal communication, May 11, 2002).

He certainly savored life. I remember he loved strawberries. And whenever he would go on a trip and strawberries were in season, he would consume vast amounts of strawberries and milk (T. Rillo, personal communication, December 27, 2001).

Both [of our] boys were babysat by L. B. My son would call him 'B. B.' or 'Bee Bee.' They would both curl up in his lap. Kevin spent his first two years of life there. They would curl up with him. We had a big old overstuffed armchair that was, I think, it was probably Loren's grandfather's. It was so old. But anyway, he would sit in that chair with one kid on [each] side and tell them stories. He loved to tell them stories (T. Rillo, personal communication, December 27, 2001).

In my early years, I didn't think about who [L. B.] was or what he was or the significance of it. Not until I was of college age did I ever realize that I was talking to a pioneer (T. Rillo, personal communication, December 27, 2001).

He was indeed the Father of Outdoor Education. . . . I was asked by someone . . . if I was the Mother of Outdoor Education and I replied, 'It depended on who the father was' (E. Roller, personal communication, January 28, 2002).

When I met him, he still had that flair and charisma that showed, even if he was just eating a meal. He had a good sense of humor. Of course, he was respected by other people, and you could see that in the reverence with which so many people treated him (P. Yambert, personal communication, March 24, 2002).

He would say when he would lean back in his chair, 'Some day, I'm going to watch and all the school buses will be going in the other direction.' He would say that a lot of times at the end of a speech. That's what he was wishing for (E. Ambry, personal communication, February 10, 2002).

—7—
L. B.'s Leadership

A portion of the analysis of the narratives for this study entailed the identification of descriptive patterns and themes pertaining to Sharp's approach to leadership. The patterns revealed more than a simple existence of aspects of leadership, such as the existence of a philosophy. Of significance, for example, was what Sharp did with his philosophy, articulating it in such a way that it was understandable and easily repeated by others. Sharp's leadership was manifest in the perpetuation of outdoor education through other people. The patterns are therefore described in terms of Sharp's leadership actions and presented by the narrators' descriptions of the influence of those actions on their personal and professional lives.

Articulation of Philosophy

Sharp's philosophy of education and of outdoor education were one and the same. His philosophy was based on the thesis that the best places and best ways to learn certain things ought to be determined and acted upon. Those things that are best learned outdoors through direct experiences should be taught that way. This philosophy exemplifies the practical dimensions of Dewey's pragmatism. Nearly every narrator recounted this basic philosophy.

One of the strongest patterns in Sharp's approach to leadership was that of having a succinct and sound philosophy of education that was easily articulated by others. The descriptions of Sharp's philosophy are consistent from person to person, and consistent with Sharp's own writing.

> [L. B.] called it spiritual uplift. . . . Your inner soul had to believe in something, and it was essential to living. Besides having food and [shelter], you had to have some kind of spiritual understanding of the world and natural features and people and kindness and all of those were kind of, if you could call it, religious (E. Ambry, personal communication, February 10, 2002).

> We focused on the outdoor activities, relating it to what was going on inside and outside the school. Everything is tied together. These things are not separate. We just go to where we can study it best (R. Christie, personal communication, May 9, 2002).

> He told the story of Admiral Byrd who was asked why he went on his explorations. His answer was, 'to explore an unknown place.' Anyway, that really captures the essence of [L. B.'s] philosophy that the out-of-doors ought to be a constant source of discovery or exploration and the program ought to be planned so that that happens. . . . The essence of [L. B.'s] philosophy was 'to explore an unknown area.' You might also call it a program principle (C. Knapp, personal communication, December 19, 2001).

> He encouraged learning through experience firsthand. He felt that you retain much more longer and more vividly than if you learned it by rote or by secondary sources. He was always in favor of direct experiences. That was his Columbia influence too as well. John Dewey was an advocate of that (T. Rillo, personal communication, December 27, 2001).

> He believed in 'education for what is real' and had the ability to help others to understand that education is more than

'2 × 4: the four walls of a classroom, and the two covers of a book.' . . . He felt that children had been looking out of windows for a long time, and that outdoor education took them there (E. Roller, personal communication, January 28, 2002).

One aspect of Sharp's philosophy articulated by the narrators was the emphasis on learning-by-doing to solve everyday problems, referred to here as *problem-based learning*. Problem-based learning has been advocated by Bridges and Hallinger (1997) as a strategy whereby solving problems of practice leads to gains in new knowledge formation. Self-directed learning and decision-making skills are enhanced through problem-based learning. Narrator Ellie Morrison expounded on Sharp's promotion of this type of learning:

> L. B. Sharp's learn-by-doing methods presented a practical approach to education at National Camp. Living and study centered the small camp set-up with campers accepting tasks and experiencing the excellence of the group process interaction while reaping the benefits of outdoor living (E. Morrison, personal communication, May 11, 2002).

The following two stories took place at Camp Raritan and are indicative of the problem-based learning philosophy that was instilled at the Life Camps and at National Camp. Larry Huntley stressed that getting help from leaders, whether from the camp administration or from the counselors, was not considered a viable solution. Problems were expected to be solved within the learning group. The stories described two problems of everyday living that surfaced and the lessons that were learned from them.

> All of our food was in a big chuck box. . . . The doors locked just to keep out predators. Well, a raccoon came in and smelled food, and he climbed up on that little ledge, and he turned the handle, and he got into the food for the next day. We decided we had to do something more so we put nails in the frame above each door. Then we turned the handle, [and put in more] nails to bar [the handle]. The raccoon got in [again.] . . . We were

getting tight on rations at that point. The rule is, you take care of yourself. You don't go back for more rations. If something happens, you deal with it. We [finally] solved the problem, but to tell you the truth, I can't remember now what it was (L. Huntley, personal communication, March 15, 2002).

We had three tepees, one for the two counselors, and then each of the others had four boys. . . . We had dug a very deep trench uphill of our camp before the boys arrived and packed it down tight, so we had a good large berm protecting us against rain. When the boys came, this was the first session of course, we told them they had to dig a ditch the same way we had to protect themselves in case of rain. Well, one group did a very good job. . . . The others . . . dug up maybe three or four inches and just turned it over loose. . . . Later in the season when the first rain came, it was [a] drencher [and] with the boys in it, all of [those boys'] beds were washed downhill toward the lower side of the tent (L. Huntley, personal communication, March 15, 2002).

Beyond articulation of a sound philosophy, a philosophy must be shared with others if it is to gain credence. Sharp believed that the application of his philosophy of outdoor education could lead to great holistic growth for children and students of all ages. He dedicated his career to the promotion of his philosophy through commitment to his career-long vision.

Commitment to Vision

Sharp's vision was for outdoor education methods of learning and teaching to be embraced and integrated into educational systems at every level. For this to happen, he realized that teachers needed to have the preparation of skills, knowledge, and confidence necessary to use outdoor education as a regular part of their teaching. Universities could help in teacher preparation in outdoor education. Sharp also realized that school administrators could both enable and hinder the fulfillment of his vision. He would need to convince them that his philosophy and vision could make a difference in the education of children.

> He dedicated his whole life to outdoor education. . . . He worked very hard. . . . He was dedicated completely (E. Ambry, personal communication, February 10, 2002).

> He was dedicated to one thing and just stayed with it. Therefore, trying to get material for a book [about him] is pretty difficult because it's very repetitive. I'm not belittling him. It's just that, that was him. He talked about that in his sleep (E. Ambry, personal communication, February 10, 2002).

> He believed in what he wanted to do. He wanted to excite people into getting involved in school camping, as it was in the beginning (C. Emanuelson, personal communication, January 21, 2002).

> [L. B.] had a creativeness and a drive and basically, a single focus, and that was to promote outdoor education. First in camps in the '30s and later that evolved into promoting outdoor education in schools. That became his life goal. Maybe success comes to anyone who focuses basically on one goal (C. Knapp, personal communication, December 19, 2001).

> He was the spirit of National Camp, characterized by his humor, wisdom, vision, and idealism (E. Morrison, personal communication, May 11, 2002).

> It was just a case of . . . giving his entire being to his job, his profession, his vocation, his dream (T. Rillo, personal communication, December 27, 2001).

Sharp set about intentionally promoting his philosophy and the vision he had for its wide application in schools through engaging in several activities discussed next.

Dissemination of Philosophy and Vision

Sharp diligently sought out ways to disseminate his philosophy and vision to others. He published widely in both refereed and non-refereed journals, books, newsletters, monographs, and brochures. Many times, these publications were produced by the organizations he established, such as National Camp and the Outdoor Education Association. He established those two organizations for the specific purpose of propagating the use of outdoor education philosophy and methods. He networked profusely with other professionals through letters, memos, telephone calls, interviews, and personal visits. He presented keynote addresses and workshops at local, regional, and national conferences. Often, he organized and hosted the conferences. He gave speeches across the country to school administrators, university faculty members, teachers, youth groups, community groups, church groups, and others interested in outdoor education. He spread his philosophy through the master plans he designed for outdoor facilities. He broadcast his philosophy and vision wherever and whenever he could.

> You can look at the educational research that was done at National Camp and New York City. . . . Every summer, he had his people do projects. He had a summation of the projects compiled into one booklet. . . . There's a whole series of those things [that go] back to the early beginnings of the people who were setting up outdoor education programs in California and other places. . . . [The compiled projects were titled] *National Camp Problems* (R. Christie, personal communication, May 9, 2002).

> He was one of the most prolific writers among the early leaders in what, at the time, was termed 'camping education.' . . . Without question, he's one of the giants of outdoor education. I think he certainly laid a philosophical groundwork for what has happened. He certainly was a disseminator through his writings, his publications, and of course, through National Camp, his teaching, and the kind of programs that he put

on for other educators and their going-out to various parts of the country and influencing many, many others. He has to be counted among some of the key people that ever existed in outdoor education. He certainly has influenced many of us and has to be admired for that (D. Hammerman, personal communication, January 6, 2002).

I think one of the secrets of good leadership is to gather good people around you and let them go to do their thing. [L. B.] did that well, even though he usually wanted to hold the reins. He never wanted to completely let people go, but he let people go when he knew they shared his philosophy and would do good things (C. Knapp, personal communication, December 19, 2001).

He had the support, the drive, the dedication, the position, and the status. He was a white male with a Ph.D. in the '30s, '40s, '50s and into the '60s who was sought out. He had power and status because he wrote and published. He studied under some of the progressive educators at Columbia University which was a high status university. He drew people who were very dedicated to him (C. Knapp, personal communication, December 19, 2001).

Various newsletters and publications permitted a continual update of the growth and development of this educational field. The Outdoor Education Association newsletter and *Extending Education* publications as well as articles, periodicals, and book reviews continually [kept me] posted relating to L. B. Sharp, professional contacts, and projects (E. Morrison, personal communication, May 11, 2002).

[L. B. arranged the production of] three films in his time. The first one [was made] in the late 1930s called 'Youth and Camps.' Then [there was] another one called 'Camping Education' which was around 1940, in that period of time. . . . The first experiment in school camping was in 1947. 'School Time and Camp' was the name of the film [that reported the school camping experiment]. . . . 'Camping Education' dealt with 1940 and opening up National Camp for adults (T. Rillo, personal communication, December 27, 2001).

[L. B. made a] pioneer effort to make the ideas acceptable to educators and the people he trained and sent out all over the country to put outdoor education into the school curriculums. L. B. made outdoor education respectable and showed through tests and studies that outdoor education can make a difference not only in science, but in other subjects in school. He inspired people to try this new approach to education and he helped many people to understand that this was a wonderful way to help some students learn and others to understand the out-of-doors (E. Roller, personal communication, January 28, 2002).

Living a Principled Life

Narrators described in detail the ways that Sharp's everyday actions were congruent with his philosophy of outdoor education and the things that he tried to teach others. He exemplified adherence to a set of principles in his personal and professional life. The descriptions offered below by the narrators indicated that Sharp exhibited a high level of ethical behavior and cared deeply for others. He also held a high regard for the natural outdoor environment and stressed that it should be treated with care.

Character and ethics. Some of the narrators described Sharp's value system in terms of character. Others portrayed it in terms of ethics.

In terms of his character, I don't think anybody could say anything except great. . . . He was a very reliable, very wonderful person (E. Ambry, personal communication, February 10, 2002).

Probably in terms of the world [of] ethics, he [had] one of the highest levels of any individual I have known. He was very much a straight-shooter, but he was also very independent. To be ethical is to be independent. You have to be a person of conviction. L. B. was very much a person of conviction, and [he] acted upon those convictions (R. Christie, personal communication, May 9, 2002).

If L. B. told you something that he was going to do or expected, . . . it would be done. It was the way he lived his life (R. Christie, personal communication, May 9, 2002).

His ethics were the highest is all I can say. I never had anything but the highest respect for him (C. Emanuelson, personal communication, January 21, 2002).

L. B. expressed an appreciation of the contribution of each staff member associated with National Camp. He encouraged leadership of all professionals relating to their unique contribution to the program (E. Morrison, personal communication, May 11, 2002).

L. B.'s performance exemplified ideal human character. He continually conformed to professional standards of conduct (E. Morrison, personal communication, May 11, 2002).

L. B. Sharp had a tolerance, an acceptance of mistakes (T. Rillo, personal communication, December 27, 2001).

I think L. B. had the greatest, the ethical values, absolutely at the highest level, amazing for a man who professed not to go to church. I know people that are churchgoers who had fewer virtues than he did (T. Rillo, personal communication, December 27, 2001).

Caring for others. The importance of care in educational leadership has been stressed in seminal works by renowned scholars such as Nel Noddings (1992), Parker Palmer (1993), and Lynn Beck (1994). In addition to being an ethical leader, Sharp cared for and about others and revealed his caring in many ways.

He was a very kind, gentle person. He was extremely thought-ful. His mind was right to the end. It was so sharp. He was aware of what was going on. He had a lot of patience in work-ing with people and kids. He had a great deal of feeling and affection for people (R. Christie, personal communication, May 9, 2002).

[He was] always a gentleman. . . . Sometimes, when he would get an audience that wasn't too prone to accept what he had, he would never get angry about it (E. Ambry, personal com-munication, February 10, 2002).

He just had a great feeling for people, and this great intellect, and great courage and independence. He would just go his own way no matter what other people thought. He knew that he was on a sound track (R. Christie, personal communica-tion, May 9, 2002).

[L. B. was] a very warm friendly person (R. Christie, personal communication, May 9, 2002).

He was a good listener (C. Emanuelson, personal communi-cation, January 21, 2002).

L. B. was a kind, considerate man interested in encouraging people to express themselves in fellowship (E. Morrison, personal communication, May 11, 2002).

He was so warm and compassionate. [My sons] were the grandchildren that he never knew. . . . He basically had every gene that said 'family,' 'father' (T. Rillo, personal communica-tion, December 27, 2001).

Care for the natural outdoor environment. Not only did Sharp display great care for others, but he cared for the natural outdoor environment as well. Sharp's ties to the land, self-admittedly, grew from his childhood experiences on a Kansas farm. It is not surpris-ing, then, that he advocated an awareness of and appreciation for the out-of-doors in his philosophy of outdoor education. His actions and his words expressed care for the outdoors and resulted in the following recollections:

> [L. B. had a] very close, a natural kinship or bonding with nature. I think he loved the natural world. He had a natural affinity for it. I think he was capable of passing that on to others and sharing it with others (D. Hammerman, personal communication, January 6, 2002).

> He never permitted people to throw trash in a fireplace that was used for campfires and ceremonies. He believed that a trash can is where you throw your trash. A sacred fire was where you only put wood. . . . He had his ways of expressing what was right and good, which is an ethical aspect (C. Knapp, personal communication, December 19, 2001).

> Each time [L. B.] wrote his report to accompany a master plan map, he would make sure that the text reflected the ethical and aesthetic treatment of the land. For example, he always recommended that buildings not be placed on a lake where they could be seen from the lake. He always wanted to preserve that aesthetic quality of being out in a canoe and looking on the shore and not seeing a structure (C. Knapp, personal communication, December 19, 2001).

> He always used a poem written by one of his campers, Joe Treu, on 'What is the night?' The poem is about the beauty of the night and not being afraid. I think he saw the out-of-doors as the source of many lessons. He wanted to have youngsters and oldsters appreciate that (C. Knapp, personal communication, December 19, 2001).

> *What is the night?*
> *A dark and fearsome thing*
> *That causes us to tremble*
> *To bend our knees and pray for light?*
> *Ah no! 'Tis beauty,*
> *'Tis beauty born of peace*
> *And rest from earthly strife*
> *A part of eternity is the beauty of the night. (Treu, 1947, p. 93)*

He encouraged kinship with the earth in all his associations (E. Morrison, personal communication, May 11, 2002).

L. B. Sharp was leading this group around, and all of a sudden, they heard this chattering of birds . . . and their shrill little sounds. There were two robins, a male and a female robin flittering around. Here was this black snake partway up the tree [that] had gotten into the nest and was eating the baby robins. So, L. B. Sharp [said], 'What would you do?' to the group that was with him. One of them said, 'Kill the snake!' And L. B. said, 'Kill the snake? . . . Is it right to kill the snake just because of what the snake is doing? . . . The snake is only doing what it was intended to do' (T. Rillo, personal communication, December 27, 2001).

Exhibiting Admirable Interpersonal Skills

Sharp possessed interpersonal skills that were highly developed and obviously respected. One aspect of Sharp's interpersonal appeal revealed through the narrative data was a strong, independent presence. In other respects, the narrators' descriptions characterized the attribute of charisma when defined as "a personal magic of leadership arousing special popular loyalty or enthusiasm" (Merriam-Webster's Collegiate Dictionary, 1993, p. 193). Although charisma in leaders may carry negative connotations in relation to coercion, power, and propaganda, Sharp's leadership was firmly grounded in his adherence to ethical behavior. Aspects of his interpersonal skills were described in terms of his presence, speaking, storytelling, and showmanship abilities.

Remarkable presence. Sharp was described as a tall man. He also usually wore a shaped felt hat that added height to his stature. His physical appearance combined with his interpersonal skills made a remarkable impression on people.

> He could be a very imposing man, yet he was one of the most un-imposing men that I ever met. He and I could get into some pretty hot discussions sometimes, as I'm prone to do and he could, but it was always on the topic. He always treated me as an equal (R. Christie, personal communication, May 9, 2002).

> L. B., I understand, could be bristly or abrasive. He needed to [be]. He would rub some of the academics the wrong way (D. Hammerman, personal communication, January 6, 2002).

> L. B. always struck me as being something of a paradox, something of a loner in one way and yet quite gregarious in other ways (D. Hammerman, personal communication, January 6, 2002).

Mainly, one way of putting it was his presence. It was not so much that he was a big man, but he was a man who called for respect just by appearance, by behavior, and of course, we all knew his reputation (L. Huntley, personal communication, March 15, 2002).

[L. B.] had a great sense of humor. . . . He was a joker. Any opportunity that he could find to joke was what he really enjoyed. But he was also a serious—you might today call him— a 'workaholic.' He was 'married' to the Outdoor Education Association, the organization that he founded (C. Knapp, personal communication, December 19, 2001).

[Descriptions of my memories of L. B. are] father figure, great sense of humor, creative showman. He loved to capture an audience and hold them in his hand. And he could do it (C. Knapp, personal communication, December 19, 2001).

[L. B.] was personable and that was one of [his] skills. He could talk anyone's language. He could talk the Ph.D.'s scholarly language, and he could talk the farmer's language. Of course, it helped that he grew up on a farm (C. Knapp, personal communication, December 19, 2001).

Public speaking abilities. Based on the previous narratives, it is not surprising that Sharp was often invited as a public speaker at conferences, workshops, and other gatherings. Most of the narrators commented on Sharp's speechmaking abilities, which they had experienced firsthand.

L. B. Sharp was very prominent, making speeches all over the country. . . . [He] spoke many, many times to school boards and to school superintendents and people at a higher level. He would come [to my home] and we would sit down and write a speech that would be given to whoever was attending these conferences. . . . He never wrote out a whole speech. He worked from outlines. We would put our heads together. Some of the superintendents I knew very well. He would use their names. We would know where some of the camps were, the school camps and things like that. We would sort of personalize it, and it was fun (E. Ambry, personal communication, February 10, 2002).

He was a very good speaker. When he had an audience of maybe 300 people, what he was talking about was coming from his heart. I never remember anybody walking out of his lectures. He was so dedicated and so sure that education could be better than what it was. Just putting people in classrooms and locking them up was not the way to educate children or adults. He stressed that, and he was sincere. He was a powerful speaker. He was convincing, because what he said made sense. Why do you have to learn everything from a book? Everything in a book was borrowed from the outside (E. Ambry, personal communication, February 10, 2002).

Storytelling and showmanship. Sharp was a storyteller who often repeated many of the same stories in order to make a point or provide a meaningful message. He would sometimes elaborate and alter his tales. Thus, some of the narrators shared different versions of the same stories, but all stressed his propensity for showmanship.

I recall [an] early meeting [at] an ACA national convention in Chicago. That was one of the first times I had heard him speak. I thought, 'What a character. What an interesting engaging character this guy is,' because he was a storyteller. He had this audience rolling in the aisles over this tale about him growing up on a farm in Kansas (D. Hammerman, personal communication, January 6, 2002).

L. B. was a showman, amongst other things. . . . In outdoor cooking, he could be 'a little bit' flamboyant. When he was making his coffee . . . we used Number 10 cans. . . . It had a wire bail we could hold. [We] put the coffee in the water and [brought] it up to a boil. Sometimes we put sticks across the top, just to break down the bubbles coming up. . . . When he had a group of leaders, he wanted to be just a little bit more flamboyant, so he would grab the bail and he would swing it in a complete 360 degree vertical arc. It would be from the ground up over his head. He would swing that thing around to use the centrifugal force to force the grounds down to the bottom of the pail. . . . I was with him one day when there was a group of church leaders that were on a log. L. B. was standing directly in front of them, about ten feet out in front of them. . . . He was swinging the pail directly at them. . . . Well, all of a sudden, this thing took off like a rocket and went over their heads. The bail broke. This was hot coffee. It never touched anybody, but it went right over their heads. . . . He just laughed (R. Christie, personal communication, May 9, 2002).

He was a showman. [In making coffee, after waving the] can around in a circular force like this . . . he would tap it on the ground three times. He would take the can and stand on one foot, one leg and heel behind the other leg. He would tip the can into his coffee cup, balanced on that one foot, and pour it in. . . . If he could do something with a story or a graphic illustration, he would do it (T. Rillo, personal communication, December 27, 2001).

He did the 'Hoya! Hoya!' bit, where he had everybody out there saying 'Hoya! Hoya!' Most people didn't know what 'Hoya, Hoya,' meant. . . . Well, 'hoya,' I forget which of the Indian tribes, but that was the term for the buffalo dung. . . . He never told them. It's just one of the things he did (R. Christie, personal communication, May 9, 2002).

He was very much a showman, but always with a tremendous twinkle in his eye. . . . He would do things that were fun, that people could laugh at, but he wasn't trying to build himself up in a special kind of image. He could be very self-depreciating. He would make fun of himself. It was that kind of sense of humor. It was a very kind sense of humor that let people be at ease (R. Christie, personal communication, May 9, 2002).

He would gather a group and say, 'I would like to conduct a symphony called the symphony of the aspens.' He would stand erect as though he were the conductor and then he would try to time his hand movements to the start of breeze that would come up the valley. That wind would shake the aspen leaves. So he would, in all the pomp and circumstance of an actor and a conductor, lead the symphony of the aspens (C. Knapp, personal communication, December 19, 2001).

There [was] a lot of humor [and] a lot of wonderful humorous stories that were associated with L. B. Those people around him also were great storytellers. Story telling was something we did around campfires. We had a campfire every evening at National Camp and at Life Camps (T. Rillo, personal communication, December 27, 2001).

Storytelling is an example of just one tradition that campers and staff engaged in together. There were other traditions and regular experiences recounted by the narrators as being very meaningful to them.

Facilitating Meaningful Experiences and Traditions

There were stories told often by the narrators of their most meaningful experiences and the various traditions that were carried on throughout the years at the Life Camps and National Camp. Singing before meals and at evening campfires, storytelling, child-led vesper services, honorary awards of recognition, and reflection through the writing and recitation of poetry were all traditions described as important by the narrators. Honorary axes were mentioned by a few of the narrators. Elizabeth Roller recalled receiving hers.

I remember one year he gave each of the small camps a "spivy" axe. This [was] a small axe—not a hand axe—that is just the right size for girls' hands. He made quite a production of it and we burned the name of the small camp, "Pioneers," on its handle (E. Roller, personal communication, January 28, 2002).

Two traditions that were repeatedly highlighted by the narrators were "buffalo throws" and evening campfires.

Buffalo Throws. A Buffalo Throw, sometimes referred to as a "Tro," was a special steak dinner that was usually served on the last night of a camp session or leadership institute. The steaks were seared and cooked directly on a large hot bed of coals. Although the meat was actually beef, tradition held that a long story would be told while the steaks were cooking that described how the buffalo meat was collected from Kansas. A detailed descriptive history of Buffalo Throws can be found in Rillo (2001).

> You start out by getting your wood. You have to have a certain amount of sawed wood, cut just so, about a foot long and an inch thick. . . . Then, you have the stages of soft wood to hard wood because when you get the fire ready for the steak, it has to be all hard wood coals at least four inches thick. So you build this fire up to that point, but then there's the matter of the steak. It takes time to get the steak because you had to get the buffalo. You didn't want to kill the buffalo. You wanted to keep them around so they could produce some more steak. So . . . you would have zippers on each side of the hind quarter and the buffalo would go up to a shagbark hickory and rub his side, and the zipper would [open and then you would] slice away a nice two-inch thick steak and zip it back up again (C. Emanuelson, personal communication, January 21, 2002).

> One of the things I learned from L. B., you can do little things. Like when he was doing the Buffalo Throw and he was using the M & M [candies]. 'This meat is going to be a little tough on your stomach, so we have this little pill to settle things down' (R. Christie, personal communication, May 9, 2002).

> It was a treat to meet L. B. and experience [a buffalo throw] and just to rub shoulders with him as we had dinner afterward. He spent the day there. It was just kind of a bonus (L. Huntley, personal communication, March 15, 2002).

He made a big issue of the marinating [of the steaks]. If the groups were there the night before, they would see him marinade the steaks. He would massage the steaks with his hands and put the oil and cloves in there. . . . Then he would tell the story [of] how he would send me or somebody out to Kansas. There was a herd of buffalo out there, and we would select the fattest, laziest-looking, succulent buffalo. We would put a notch in the ear of the buffalo, and then we'd come home. When it was time to go back for the buffalo, he'd send me out again, or somebody like me, and then we would get the buffalo meat. In the meantime, the guy that had the buffalo herd would put the one selected in a stall, and he would feed it the best of grain. Classical music would be played to [the buffalo] so it would mellow and the meat would be just right (T. Rillo, personal communication, December 27, 2001).

The Buffalo 'Tro' began with Ernest Thompson Seton, and he got it from the Plains Indians who would cook their steaks using buffalo chips. . . . [L. B.] would dip [the steaks] in this oil and butter. . . . Then we would slice it on the bias, and serve it that way. . . . You burned at least . . . a pickup truck full of hard wood. You would burn that fire all day long (T. Rillo, personal communication, December 27, 2001).

Campfires. Sharp viewed fires, specifically campfires, as a sacred part of the outdoor experience. Campfires were a part of the evening program at each of the small group living sites as well as a part of each large gathering or ceremony.

As you know, L. B. was quite a showman. He made a big deal out of campfires. He would go through the ceremony always burning the ashes of the last fire that they had during the summer season at his Life Camps. Then, the next year at the first fire, they would dig up the ashes from last year's fire to establish the continuity. Chestnut was a real fine burning wood so he would use that to start the fires and then tell the story of the chestnut to the open-jawed students that were listening (P. Yambert, personal communication, March 24, 2002).

The tradition [was] a campfire program at the end of every day. Well, on a rainy evening, we couldn't have a campfire. . . . We moved into one of the boys' tepees and had our campfire there in the circle. . . . We put a match in the middle of the tent and that was our campfire when we sang our closing song (L. Huntley, personal communication, March 15, 2002).

One time I went on a workshop with [L. B.] in Ohio. . . . He then decided that that would be the celebration of his four-thousandth tepee fire. . . . Then, I started to think about, 'Well, what does that mean? Four thousand tepee fires. How many years does that reflect spent in a tepee?' That was a lot of years when you think about it. Most of the time he couldn't do it year-round. It probably was mostly during the summers. So, what if he got ninety days a year? . . . That's more than 44 years he spent in the tepee (C. Knapp, personal communication, December 19, 2001).

L. B. Sharp had the . . . concept of a fire, the unification, the sense of identity, the sense of tie-in with safety and security and home. Wherever you go, with a fire, you're at home (T. Rillo, personal communication, December 27, 2001).

Sharp's Influence on Perpetuating Outdoor Education Through Others

This chapter has thus far described patterns of Sharp's leadership actions including creating and disseminating a philosophy and vision, living a principled life, exhibiting admirable interpersonal skills, and facilitating meaningful traditions and experiences. Beyond describing Sharp's action, the narrators also described the impressions that Sharp's leadership made on people and expressed those impressions in two main ways: in terms of their own lives and their decisions to perpetuate outdoor education in some faction of their own careers, and also in terms of Sharp's influence that they had observed in persons other than themselves.

Influence on self. The following series of narratives describe ways that the nine narrators, all of whom carried out careers in various arenas of outdoor education, saw Sharp's leadership influence play out in their own lives.

> I had a full program to be on the campus [at Montclair State College] all of the time, but when I would break away and I would have time or take a small leave or something like that, I would get back into what L. B. Sharp was doing, if he was having a conference or something like that (E. Ambry, personal communication, February 10, 2002).

> When I was at Northern Illinois University, I was invited to come down for a summer to teach at the University of Cincinnati. . . . I was asked to teach "The Future of Education". . . . This was in the '60s. . . . I had superintendents and principals from big cities. . . . When the course ended, almost unanimously, they said, 'This is the first course we've ever had that was taught the way an education course should be taught.' [In] examining what they were doing . . . and how society was changing and how people were changing, we were working this out using the brain power of the group which is a massive force if it can be capitalized upon. Essentially, this all goes back to L. B. This is what he wanted for the kids at camp, in working things out. . . . This is what he was all about— getting people to use their minds to discover, explore, to have the freedom to do this . . . doing that exploratory kind of work and the reasoning in working things out (R. Christie, personal communication, May 9, 2002).

> [At one] time, I was working with communities . . . in developing open space plans and conferences for teacher training . . . throughout the country. . . . Several communities wanted to . . . get involved in environmental education, not specifically outdoor education or school camping, because the name was switching during that time to more environmental concerns. Wherever I could, I tried to work in the school camping and outdoor education part of it, too (C. Emanuelson, personal communication, January 21, 2002).

One thing that I would say that grew out of [my association with L. B.] was my concern with wanting to keep environmental areas, open space areas in the communities (C.
Emanuelson, personal communication, January 21, 2002).

L. B. and I never personally worked together . . . nor did I
ever actually study with him. Nevertheless, he did have a
very strong influence on me philosophically, mainly from my
study of his early publications. . . . I did draw a great bit from
L. B. in terms of the early development of school camping
for [my] dissertation (D. Hammerman, personal communication, January 6, 2002).

I give Life Camps credit for so many of the successes in my
career working with church young people. The skills and
knowledge I learned there just worked everywhere I went,
dealing with troubled kids, bringing kids out. It just set me
up for a lifetime career that I was moving into and prepared
me beautifully for it. I'm very grateful for that, and I'm not
the only one that has expressed that kind of feeling for what
they learned (L. Huntley, personal communication, March
15, 2002).

I became a teacher after four years of college. In my teaching,
I tried to use the outdoors whenever possible. I was a science
teacher at first. . . . I helped students build a nature trail and
a weather station on the school property. We also planted
trees. Wherever I could integrate the out-of-doors with my
science, I did (C. Knapp, personal communication, December
19, 2001).

L. B. Sharp influenced my personal and professional life from
my association with him as executive director at National
Camp in the summer of 1948 to the present time as I continually become involved in programs, projects, and reviews
relating to camping education. . . . I treasure the memories
and continue sharing the educational message of [my National Camp] adventure (E. Morrison, personal communication, May 11, 2002).

This man has had an influence on my life. He shaped my career among others, but principally him. He was very influential in my focusing on outdoor education as a career. I feel privileged to have known him (T. Rillo, personal communication, December 27, 2001).

Sharp's influence on others. The narrators readily shared the influence that Sharp had on them. They just as enthusiastically explained their observations of ways Sharp had influenced other people. The persons named below were also outdoor educators and followers of Sharp's philosophy.

[L. B.] got a lot of other people to do a lot of writing (E. Ambry, personal communication, February 10, 2002).

He was building up a cadre of people that extended throughout the country like myself (C. Emanuelson, personal communication, January 21, 2002).

He had a strong following. People who had attended National Camps were very devoted to him. It was almost like L. B. and his 'disciples.' . . . They adored the man, almost worshipped him, and understandably. He had great personal impact on these people (D. Hammerman, personal communication, January 6, 2002).

When you think about the hundreds, perhaps thousands, of people that he influenced particularly through National Camp, and the National Camp Problems that were carried out . . . (D. Hammerman, personal communication, January 6, 2002).

My first camp director at the [New Jersey State] School of Conservation was Tom Rillo, who had been to National Camp and just worshipped L. B. Sharp, as many people did (C. Knapp, personal communication, December 19, 2001).

[Tom Rillo is] one of the 'disciples.' He sees L. B. right up there on the pedestal, as he ought to be (D. Hammerman, personal communication, January 6, 2002).

National Camp was a camp for adults, primarily teachers who came . . . for six weeks. They would work on a problem that related to the implementation of a camping education program in their respective school systems. Believe me, the evidence was there: San Diego with Camp Cuyamaca [and] Los Angeles with Camp High Hill. These camps started in former CCC sites, Civilian Conservation Corps, and were taken over by school systems. These teachers [who came went on to become] coordinators of outdoor education in their respective places: North Carolina, New York State, everywhere you look (T. Rillo, personal communication, December 27, 2001).

[Ann Brinley] was devoted to him. . . . She would spend her entire summers working for him. She was a friend and a counselor who really embraced the outdoor education concept (T. Rillo, personal communication, December 27, 2001).

Rey Carlson was here [at Indiana University]. . . . He contacted me and said, 'I'm retiring, and I'd like for you to apply for my job because you and I have the same background and the same philosophy.' . . . He came here in 1946 to Indiana University. In 1945, '46, '47, '48, Rey Carlson was a faculty member at National Camp (T. Rillo, personal communication, December 27, 2001).

There was a gentleman by the name of Dr. Leslie Holmes at Northern Illinois University. He was the university president [and] attended a conference that L. B. Sharp . . . spoke at with E. DeAlton Partridge and others. . . . When he heard L. B. talk, he was so influenced [to begin the Lorado Taft Field Campus for Outdoor Teacher Education]. . . . What an influence there, L. B. Sharp being a catalyst for [this] major teacher preparation institution in the country (T. Rillo, personal communication, December 27, 2001).

L. B. had taught at National Camp the people who went out and started programs in their own states. . . . L. B.'s influence on these people made outdoor education known throughout the country (E. Roller, personal communication, January 28, 2002).

Correlation of Sharp's Leadership with Current Leadership Theory

There are many facets of Sharp's leadership that appear in the past and current body of leadership literature. Early emphasis on trait theory, for example, revealed that physical characteristics such as tall stature and an attractive appearance were evident in people (usually males) who were described as effective leaders (Northouse, 2007). Sharp was described as a tall, attractive man. Later views of trait theory, such as those espoused by Stogdill (1974), concentrated on desirable personality traits. Assertiveness, self-confidence, ambitiousness, integrity, and sociability are traits that have been attributed to Sharp by his associates and identified as leadership traits by Stogdill. McCall and Lombardo (1983) advocated that admirable interpersonal skills were also indicative of success for leaders. The narrators of this study confirmed that Sharp had highly developed, even charismatic, interpersonal abilities.

Followership is a growing topic in leadership studies that can certainly be correlated to Sharp's leadership. Sergiovanni (1996; 2006) investigated the reciprocal benefits that leaders and followers gained from each other. Leader/follower relationships were often found, in retrospect, as having high degrees of mutual respect that elevated the level of moral behavior and aspiration for both parties. Sergiovanni also closely associated followership with shared vision. In most leadership situations where followership was high, there was also the existence of a shared vision at the center of the organization or endeavor.

It is an easy bridge to construct between Sharp and various historical and current leadership approaches. Perhaps the best characterization of Sharp's leadership in relation to established leadership theory is that of transformational leadership (Burns, 1978; Bass, 1985). Burns found that people described as transformational by followers usually exhibited many of the attributes described above such as charisma, interpersonal abilities, and high integrity. Burns posited transformational leadership as a process or interplay between leaders and followers, rather than a prescriptive model. Transformational leadership emerges as *a posteriori* descriptions of effective leadership by those people who were influenced by it. When people "look back" at leaders who were transformational for them, they describe moral leaders who helped convert them from followers to leaders themselves—as leaders who were concerned with helping them reach their full potential (Stewart, 2006). They were viewed as visionary and oriented toward long-

term goals. They were leaders who adhered to values, ethical behavior, high expectations, and standards.

Bass (1985; 1990) validated and extended Burns' (1978) theory of transformational leadership through conducting multiple research studies with U.S. military officers. Bass confirmed four dimensions that must be prevalent for transformational leadership to occur: charisma or idealized influence, inspiration or inspirational motivation, intellectual stimulation, and individualized consideration. All four of these were evident in the narratives provided by those who were interviewed relative to the influence Sharp had on them.

L. B. Sharp did have a charismatic personality shaped by his remarkable physical presence, his story-telling and speech-making abilities, his principled living, and his unwavering sense of purpose. Sharp also inspired and motivated others to follow in his footsteps or carve their own paths in outdoor education and leadership. He also provided intellectual stimulation through his emphasis on scholarship and problem-solving for the students involved with National Camp. Each student completed a research paper during each leadership course that presented an actual plan for integrating outdoor education into a new or existing program. These papers, bound as an annual book series entitled *National Camp Problems*, were published from 1940 until 1951. Furthermore, Sharp was described as giving individualized consideration to everyone he encountered, from company executives to cafeteria workers. He provided a respectful and accepting aura that permeated throughout the organizations he led.

More current research by Kouzes and Posner (2002) examined transformational leadership through the perspective of leaders and their descriptions of successful experiences. They developed a set of five practices that exemplary leaders tend to exhibit: modeling the way, inspiring a shared vision, challenging the process, enabling others to act, and encouraging the heart. Leaders clearly express and personally model their values and expectations. Leaders remain committed to their vision and inspire others to join them, and work toward attaining their own vision and dreams. Challenging the process involves being willing to adapt and take risks into unknown territory based on new learning. Effective leaders enable others to act by building trust, confidence, respect, support, and collaboration. Transformational leaders also recognize, praise, and reward others for their accomplishments. They use ceremony and ritual to build collective ownership, identity, and spirit. These five practices are all evident in the behaviors and actions of L. B. Sharp.

Although the portrayal of transformational leadership above is primarily positive and an approach to which many of us would like to ascribe, there are some criticisms of the approach that also emerged to some degree in relation to Sharp's leadership. One of these is the tendency for followers to display behaviors associated with hero worship (Northouse, 2007). Some of the narrators for the study were able, as mature adults, to see and articulate weaknesses in Sharp's leadership in this regard. His desires and needs were sometimes the focal point, rather than those of his followers. He had such a strong presence and followership that his passing resulted in a definite loss of momentum and eventual end to many of the endeavors in which he had begun.

Although none of the narrators used the term *transformational* in reference to Sharp, there is no doubt that their words reveal a leader who was transformational for them and for countless others, too. People were attracted to Sharp because he cared for them and touched their hearts in a special, personal way. He asked them to share in his vision of bringing children to the outdoors for the purpose of benefiting both people and the environment. He led by example and worked tirelessly side-by-side with people toward the long-term goal of outdoor education being an integral part of the regular school curriculum. Through his leadership, he inspired people to accomplish more than they thought possible, and to work toward a greater good for the planet and its children. In so doing, he transformed American education along the way.

— *8* —

Epilogue

Outdoor Education Today

As discussed earlier in the book, L. B. Sharp promoted outdoor education as an extension of the school curriculum, using outdoor experiences to teach traditional subjects such as mathematics, language arts, music, art, science, and history. Although fellow outdoor educator Julian Smith also included outdoor recreational activities into his parameters of outdoor education, both men viewed outdoor education as integrated with the educational aims of schools. When Sputnik, the first satellite, was launched by Russia in 1957, widespread concern was raised that the United States had a "pedagogically soft" (Gutek, 1991, p. 109) school curricula. Public and government entities responded with pressure on schools to increase achievement, especially in math and science. This resulted in new interest in innovative and alternative education approaches that claimed to help students learn in new ways. A period of time then ensued when new avenues of national funding for outdoor education became available (Donaldson & Donaldson, 1982).

Outdoor programs also become more school-like and less camp-like. There was less involvement of students in the planning of the outdoor education programs in which they participated. Instructional programs became more structured, scheduled, and standardized. Facilities were referred to as schools in the woods and outdoor schools rather than camps. An example was Clear Lake Camp in Michigan, one of the country's original residential outdoor education facilities. Its name was changed to the Battle Creek Outdoor Education Center around that time period (Donaldson & Donaldson, 1982).

Many of these programs and approaches also introduced new terminology professing their unique design or specific focus such as environmental education, conservation education, adventure education, experiential education, and outdoor recreation. The term outdoor education was and still is sometimes used interchangeably with these other names. One of these in particular, environmental education, was a branch that emerged as a result of the heightened environmental concern brought to light by Rachel Carson's (1962) *Silent Spring*. Carson exposed the detrimental affect that the pesticide DDT was wreaking on the offspring of Bald Eagles. Carson concluded that increasing numbers of softened, un-hatched eagle eggs were due to the pesticide washing into waterways and ingested by fish, the primary diet of the eagles. The book spawned national concern over environmental quality and served as a catalyst for the integration of environmentally focused objectives into outdoor education programs (Chavez, 1995).

In the years to follow Sputnik and *Silent Spring*, various groups offering programs that were not connected to schools or school curricula adopted the term *outdoor education*. Today, outdoor education is used often and freely to describe almost any learning experience that takes place outdoors, and to a lesser extent, learning experiences that are focused on outdoor-related topics or content. For example, a hike through a state park for senior citizens, a wilderness expedition for college credit, a church day-camp program, and an indoor lesson for a Girl Scout troop on leaf identification might all be described as outdoor education, regardless of the existence of educational-related objectives or where the events take place.

L. B. Sharp would certainly object to the attachment of the name *outdoor education* to many current programs and the various ways it is used today. On the other hand, I believe he would heartily applaud those programs that increase awareness of and reverence for the out-of-doors. He loved children and he loved the outdoors, and he would not have protested programs that brought the two into close relationship.

The Future of the Research on L. B. Sharp

At some point during this research process, it became time to write the book and cease adding more information to it. However, I view the accrual of knowledge about L. B. Sharp and the history of outdoor education as ongoing endeavors that I will be involved in throughout my own life journey. There are some areas to which I hope to give more attention and time in the future. My recommendations for continued research or related activity are discussed in the following paragraphs.

Strengthening evidence of the Dewey-Sharp connection. One of my recommendations is to continue building the connection of John Dewey's relationship to and influence on L. B. Sharp and the philosophy of outdoor education. A disappointment in the investigation into the "L. B. Sharp Papers" was the lack of direct evidence of Sharp's relationship to John Dewey. Although Sharp and his associates have established that Sharp studied under Dewey and applied Deweyan philosophy to learning in the outdoors, archival evidence to support this was not found. After several weeks of clearing obstacles presented by Teachers College-Columbia University, some partial transcripts of Sharp were finally obtained from his doctoral work there. They revealed courses taken from William Heard Kilpatrick, but not from John Dewey. I was unable to obtain Sharp's master's degree transcripts, but I will attempt to do so again at some point in the future.

The "L. B. Sharp Papers" contain both Sharp's personal and professional files. Original research papers written by Sharp for his master's degree at Teachers College-Columbia University were located. Some of the documents pertaining to Sharp's doctoral dissertation were located. Thousands of professional and personal letters, memos, and documents sent over a forty-five-year period between Sharp and his family, friends, and associates were located. Based on the extensive collection of correspondence that Sharp maintained in his files throughout his career, I anticipated that evidence of correspondence with and graduate studies under John Dewey would be found in the collection. However, as mentioned previously, these were not located.

Although the location is unknown, it is my belief that such documents revealing Sharp's and Dewey's relationship and connection do exist. It is recommended that a continual effort be made to locate documents that strengthen the Sharp-Dewey connection. Such findings will help to confirm that outdoor education was one of the few successful examples of applied Deweyan philosophy.

A need for processing the SIU collection. A rather significant hindrance to the collection of archival data for this study was the current unprocessed condition of the "L. B. Sharp Papers" held in the Special Collections of the Morris Library at Southern Illinois University in Carbondale, Illinois. The collection was not processed in the years following Sharp's death in 1963 perhaps due to health concerns of Delyte Morris, the president of SIU who brought Sharp to the university.

Morris was the university president until 1970, seven years after Sharp's death. However, during those years, Morris' mental health status steadily deteriorated until he was finally removed from his position (Mitchell, 1988; P. Yambert, personal communication, March 24, 2002). When a new SIU president was hired, and changes were made in the future plans for the Little Grassy outdoor education area, what was left of the L. B. Sharp Memorial

Library there was boxed and put in storage at the Morris Library where it has remained for over four decades.

Although the "L. B. Sharp Papers" have not been processed, a partial handwritten inventory was constructed in 1987 by Jay Fine, whose doctoral dissertation researched Sharp's design criteria for outdoor education facilities. Without Fine's inventory notes, the archival research process for this study would have taken much longer than it did. One recommendation is for the Sharp collection to be processed in such a way as to organize the thousands of loose papers into easily located bound documents, with an accompanying index for locating the contents. However, many of the documents are fragile and in deteriorating condition. At this point in technology advancements, scanning of the documents may be the easiest and most affordable avenue for continuing the collection and making it more accessible for researchers.

Annotated bibliography of Sharp's works. A third recommendation is for the creation of an annotated bibliography of Sharp's works. His publications are extensive. Transcripts from speeches, presentations, films, and interviews are available. Beyond providing a collection of Sharp's works, the bibliography would serve as an important research tool in analyzing and tracing the evolvement of Sharp's philosophy of outdoor education.

A place for the preservation of artifacts. A final recommendation, or wish perhaps, is that an appropriate place can be located some day soon for the display of countless artifacts from the outdoor education movement as well as personal items from Sharp's life and career. Many of the narrators for this study, and numerous others who have been consulted along the way, possess documents, photographs, and physical items that provide further archival evidence of the stories told in these pages. Most of the people who have these artifacts are retired and have a desire to turn these things over to someone or someplace where they can be viewed by the public, admired for their place in history, and continue to be well taken care of. Without such a place secured within the next decade, I fear relatives who are unaware of their significance will discard many of these items.

Closing Thoughts

During one of my visits to Southern Illinois University's Touch of Nature Environmental Center (originally the Little Grassy Lake Campus), I was shown an odd-shaped piece of wood, supposedly American chestnut, with names and words wood-burned into it. The names belonged to a group of children who had attended one of L. B.'s programs long ago. The words were a common phrase of his that surfaced several times during my research, a phrase that aptly describes my hopes to provide L. B. his rightful place in the history of American education and his hopes to see outdoor education integrated into schools everywhere. The words burned into the wood were simply, "Never finished, just begun."

Appendix A

About the Narrators

The following descriptions of each of the nine main narrators for this study are by no means thorough biographical sketches. These people led long and expansive careers in various genres of outdoor education, and the briefs below cannot begin to detail all that they accomplished. They were all dedicated practitioners, leaders, and pathfinders. Collectively, they hold lengthy academic credentials. They were prolific writers, theorists, creators of educative material in mountainous proportions, authors of numerous books, and heavy contributors to the scholarly knowledge in the experiential education arena. The information below describes how and when they first met L. B. Sharp, as well as information they provided during their interviews regarding their own personal journey into their careers in outdoor education.

Dr. Edward J. Ambry

Ed Ambry knew L. B. Sharp longer and had a closer relationship with him than any of the other narrators who were interviewed. In 1938, Ed was working at a company in the east that handled shipments of building materials. He noticed a large shipment that was due to be transported to a new camp (Girls' Camp) being built in Sussex County in New Jersey. Ed wrote down the name and address on the shipment and called L. B. Sharp in New York City to arrange for an interview. Ed met L. B. and began working as a counselor for Life Camps the following year, a job he returned to for many summers both before and after serving in the military during World War II. He worked with other summer programs, as well, such as the YMCA and the Boy Scouts. In later years, Ed's wife, Marge, and their three daughters were also involved in working at Life Camps and National Camp.

Ed became a teacher and went on to earn his master's degree from New York University. He served as a superintendent of schools before being invited in 1951 to become a faculty member at Montclair State College in New Jersey. While there, he authored a legislative state bill that required all teacher preparation students at the six state colleges to attend outdoor leadership training. As a part of his faculty position, Ed served five years as the director of the New Jersey State School of Conservation where the teacher trainings took place. When Ed became the dean of Graduate Studies at Montclair, Cliff Emanuelson became the director at the NJSSC. Ed was heavily involved in developing environmental education curricula for school children.

Just prior to L. B. relocating to Southern Illinois University, Ed had been working on his doctorate degree through New York University. L. B. was an NYU faculty member and the chair of Ed's dissertation committee. After L. B. moved to Carbondale, Ed took a one-year leave of absence to transfer to SIU and attend doctoral studies there. L. B. passed away before he graduated. Ed finished his doctoral studies after returning to Montclair, where he stayed for the duration of his career. Ed had been involved for several years as an officer for the Outdoor Education Association. After L. B. passed away, Ed was instrumental in carrying on the activities and mission of the association, including helping to complete unfinished surveys that L. B. had started. Ed was an enthusiastic, passionate, and valuable contributor to this study. I am grateful for the many historical artifacts he gave to me from his own collection. Ed unfortunately passed away in 2007. I deeply regret that this book was not completed before his death.

Dr. Robert M. Christie

Bob Christie well remembers his first introduction to L. B. Sharp in an elevator in New York City. He was working on his master's degree at Springfield College in Massachusetts in the mid-1950s. He and his wife, Carol, had traveled to New York City during their honeymoon, and while there, had arranged an interview with L. B. for a position at National Camp. Bob recollected that . . . "he was a charming individual. Of course, he had to hug the bride . . . ." The Christies were hired and worked at National Camp the summer of 1956 at the Matamoras, Pennsylvania, location.

Later, while a physical education teacher in Scarsdale, New York, Bob sometimes assisted L. B. in teaching some of his courses through New York University, where L. B. was on faculty. He moved to a classroom teaching position in Yorktown Heights, New York, around the same time that L. B. was arranging to move to Southern Illinois University in Carbondale in the late 1950s. In 1962, Bob was hired to establish an outdoor program at Antioch State University in Geneseo, New York. Antioch wanted Bob to attain his Ph.D. to continue his position there. Consequently, Bob arranged to move to SIU to work on his doctorate with L. B. for the fall of 1963. Unfortunately, L. B. passed away near the end of that semester, and Bob continued his doctoral studies for the new few years under Tom Rillo. Bob then went to teach for Northern Illinois University at the Lorado Taft Field Campus for three years before returning to SIU to finish his doctoral degree.

In the early 1970s, Bob was hired as the director of the Center for Environmental Outdoor Education at Bemidji State University in Minnesota and continued there for the remainder of his career. He is one of the co-founders of the Wilderness Education Association, established in 1977, with Frank Lupton, Paul Petzoldt, and Chuck Gregory. The WEA was founded out of a desire to help create competent and ethical outdoor leaders. The WEA program offers an 18-point experiential curriculum focused on judgment and decision-making.

Clifford E. Emanuelson

Cliff first met L. B. Sharp in the late 1940s while attending Springfield College in Massachusetts. Through his studies there in physical education, he attended National Camp with a group of other Springfield students. The following summer, he and his wife, Ginger, were hired as National Camp staff members. His career background includes the Los Angeles Recreation Department; the Salesmanship Club's Camp Woodland Springs; a master's degree in education; the Ridgewood, New Jersey, public school district; the New Jersey State School of Conservation; the Conservation Foundation; and the Pinchot Institute for Conservation Studies.

Through his teaching position in Ridgewood, New Jersey, Cliff initiated residential outdoor education experiences for the sixth-grade students from his school district at the New Jersey State School of Conservation. After a few years, his teaching position was changed to that of coordinating the outdoor education, science, and science curricula for the district. Soon after, he followed Edward Ambry as the director of the New Jersey State School of Conservation, and served in that position for five years, during which time the facilities were winterized for year-round programming.

Cliff then worked as an open space community planner for the Conservation Foundation in Connecticut, which led into being the associate director of the Pinchot Institute in Milford, Pennsylvania. The Institute, operating as branch of the U.S. Forest Service, also worked in partnership with the Conservation Foundation. When the Pinchot Institute eventually ended their partnership with the Conservation Foundation, Cliff became the director of the 1,300-acre Devil's Den Preserve in Weston, Connecticut. Cliff was instrumental in securing grant monies and establishing the Preserve as an educational conservation area through the Conservation Foundation and Nature Conservancy. He remained as director there for the remainder of his career. As of the time Cliff was interviewed for this study, he still carried out a tradition of hosting a Buffalo Throw on his birthday.

Dr. Donald R. Hammerman

Don's interest in outdoor education stemmed back to his youth and being involved with the Boy Scouts. During his college years, studying to be a teacher, he worked summers with YMCA summer camps, sometimes in director positions. Later, while teaching in the Bethesda, Maryland, area and earning his master's degree, he researched school camping and first learned of L. B. Sharp through his writings on outdoor education. Around the early 1950s, he applied for a position at Life Camps, and was offered a contract, but instead elected to wait for a fulltime position at the Clear Lake Camps in Battle Creek, Michigan. Don worked for three years at Clear Lake. Leslie Clark, who had been a National Camper, was the director of Clear Lake Camp during Don's first year there. Don went from the Michigan program to Northern Illinois University to work with outdoor teacher preparation there through the newly opened Lorado Taft Field Campus. He began there first as the educational director in 1954, then became the campus director and the chair of the Outdoor Teacher Education Department in 1965. He resigned as campus director and department chair in the late 1970s, but remained on faculty at NIU until he retired in 1991. Although he claims he never regretted his decision, he did state, "I've often wondered since then, if I had made that decision [to go to Life Camps], how my career might have differed or where I might have wound up."

Don first met L. B. at a national conference that was held while he was still working at Clear Lake Camp. He especially wanted to and was able to observe L. B.'s use of the Socratic method of questioning that National Camp promoted, and also to see L. B. lead a vesper service "for which he was known," which Don described as inspirational. Don and L. B. maintained a professional friendship throughout their mutual careers. In Don's doctoral dissertation from Pennsylvania State University on the historical socio-cultural influences on camping education, he acknowledged L. B.'s influence on him.

Shortly before his death in 1963, L. B. wrote the foreword for the first edition of one of Don's well-known books, *Teaching in the Outdoors*, co-authored with his wife, Elizabeth, and his brother, Bill. The second edition of the book, published after L. B.'s death, was dedicated to him.

Rev. Larry Huntley

Larry Huntley first became acquainted with L. B. through his work as a counselor at Camp Raritan for boys, one of the Life Camps located in New Jersey. He worked there for a few years around the late 1940s and early 1950s. While at Raritan, Larry served as co-counselor with the first black counselor hired by the camp. Larry also had an opportunity to be involved with one of the first sessions that National Camp offered for church camp leaders. He also worked a summer as a staff member at National Camp.

Larry's career was as an ordained minister. He recollected several special stories from implementing outdoor educational experiences for the youth in a parish he served early in his career in New Hampshire. He based much of that program on National and Life Camp practices. He claimed, "I give Life Camps credit for so many of the successes in my career working with church young people. The skills and knowledge I learned there just worked everywhere I went," and "It just set me up for a lifetime career that I was moving into and prepared me beautifully for it."

Dr. Clifford E. Knapp

While studying to become a certified teacher at Patterson State College in New Jersey, Cliff took a course called "Camping Education" which entailed attending the New Jersey State School of Conservation in the late 1950s. This was his first introduction to outdoor education. Cliff worked as a staff member the following summer at the NJSSC and Camp Wapalanne, which at the time, was being directed by Tom Rillo. During that summer, Cliff had the opportunity to travel across the Delaware River to visit Pole Bridge Camp in Matamoras, Pennsylvania, and meet L. B. Sharp.

Cliff went on to become a high school science teacher, where he incorporated outdoor education into his teaching whenever possible. This was around the same time that L. B. had relocated to Southern Illinois University. Cliff knew that Tom Rillo had followed L. B. to SIU to study under him there. Cliff decided to also move to SIU to earn his master's degree in educational administration and supervision while working as a graduate assistant under L. B. He was also involved in the reconstruction of Pole Bridge Camp at the Little Grassy Lake Campus and the first residential outdoor education programs that took place there during the summer of 1962.

After graduating from SIU, Cliff moved to the Bronx in New York to teach elementary science. That was the year that L. B. passed away and Tom Rillo was hired to carry on L. B.'s work at SIU. Cliff was hired in 1964 as the assistant coordinator of the Outdoor Education Center for Southern Illinois to help with that endeavor. He stayed there until 1972, when he was hired as the outdoor education and science specialist for the Ridgewood, New Jersey, school district, coordinating residential outdoor education programs for various grade levels throughout the district while also teaching science. While at Ridgewood, Cliff was invited to help teach at a national workshop for teachers at the Lorado Taft Field Campus, Northern Illinois University. Through attending the workshop in 1979, Cliff learned of and applied for the dual position of director of the Field Campus and chair of the outdoor education faculty at NIU. He was hired for that position in 1980 and remained there for the duration of his career until 2001.

Eleanor (Ellie) R. Morrison

Ellie first met L. B. in 1948 when she was a student at National Camp and he was the director. At this time, National Camp was located across Lake Mashipacong from the Girls' Camp. She was enrolled as a student through New York University and recalled the

National Camp Problem that she was required to complete as a part of the course. The focus of her study was on motivating students of a women's college to integrate outdoor education with other curriculum areas. Her relationship with L. B. continued throughout her career. She would often see him at conferences and other meetings, such as the annual American Camping Association conference, where L. B. often presented.

A few years after attending National Camp, Ellie earned her master's degree through Illinois State Normal College and wrote her thesis on a suggested approach for including camping education in college courses. She went to work in 1951 for a new outdoor program in Louisville, Kentucky, and patterned it after the National Camp model. She was then invited to work as the first female naturalist at Turkey Run State Park in Indiana. She used the National Camp model with that program as well. In 1953, Ellie relocated to the Cincinnati area where she developed a long career working with various youth organizations including the YWCA, Camp Fire Girls, Girl Scouts, county parks, nature centers, summer camps, and outdoor education school programs. At one time, she connected with Reynold Carlson, National Camper, to conduct a study for one of the programs she worked with. After her retirement, she remained active in numerous organizations. Sadly, Ellie passed away on September 1, 2005, "after a full life of 86 years" (D. Knoop, personal communication, September 13, 2005).

Dr. Thomas J. Rillo

Tom was born in Summit, New Jersey, and recalled childhood days spending time in the outdoors. He was especially influenced by his fifth-grade teacher, who took the students exploring in the woodlands behind his school. As a child, he was given a scholarship from a civic group in Summit to attend Camp Raritan in Pottersville, New Jersey. Tom first met L. B. there in 1938. He attended Raritan for one summer, and is the only narrator for this study who attended any of the Life Camps as a camper.

In college, Tom attended Panzer College, a specialized school for physical education in East Orange, New Jersey. Camping institutes were built into the freshman and sophomore years. Tom attended institutes that were held at the newly reopened New Jersey State School of Conservation and had opportunities to meet L. B. again through his Panzer classes. Tom worked a few summers as a counselor at the NJSSC in the early 1950s, with Ed Ambry as the director at the time. Later, in 1957, Tom served as the children's camp director there. Tom had also helped Ed Ambry with some YMCA camping programs using the decentralized concept at a facility that later became Frost Valley YMCA, one of the largest outdoor education facilities still operating in the United States.

Some years later, Tom was hired as a faculty member at Montclair State College in New Jersey. During that time, he often worked and helped with weekend and summer courses held at National Camp at the Pole Bridge site. After a ten-year relationship with National Camp, Tom took a leave of absence in 1960 from Montclair to pursue his doctoral studies at Southern Illinois University, with L. B. as the chair of his dissertation committee. Tom was back working at Montclair when L. B. passed away, and was subsequently hired by SIU in 1964 to return to fill L. B.'s position there as professor and director of the Little Grassy Lake Campus. He hired Clifford Knapp as the assistant director. Tom remained at SIU until 1967 and took a position at Glassboro State College. When Reynold Carlson, a previous National Camp staff member, retired from Indiana University in 1972, Tom was hired to replace him, and remained as a faculty member at IU until his retirement as professor emeritus.

Elizabeth (Lib) Roller

Elizabeth met L. B. Sharp during the 1940s while she was employed as a counselor at the Girls' Camp site at Lake Mashipacong. National Camp during those years was located across the lake from Girls' Camp, and L. B. often came over from National Camp to facilitate inservices or visit. Sometimes the Girls' Camp staff would spend time over at National Camp as well. Elizabeth worked there for six years. Later in Elizabeth's career as as coordinator of Environmental/Outdoor Education in Nashville, Tennessee, she saw L. B. often during a time when he was helping a local Methodist church start a decentralized camp concept.

Elizabeth's career in outdoor education began with her college studies in health and physical education at Peabody College, and later for graduate school in outdoor education and recreation (the first master's degree in the U.S. in outdoor education, according to Elizabeth). She also was prepared in special education at Peabody College. She taught in higher education for five years at Florida Southern College and Brevard College in North Carolina. Her career then launched into 10 years of teaching special education with the Nashville Metro Schools, followed by 26 years as the coordinator of Environmental & Outdoor Education for the school district. She was awarded the Conservation Educator of the Year award in Tennessee in 1971 and the Environmental Educator of the Year in Tennessee in 1986. Elizabeth is now active in archaeology and has been given a Lifetime Achievement Award from the Tennessee Professional Archaeologists of Tennessee. She still presents historical programs on American Indians and pioneers. She is also the author of several teacher manuals and booklets pertaining to outdoor environmental education.

Appendix B

Heart-of-the-Hills View Poem

So, we have, over the years named it—
  Not all at once, but gradually, increasingly, year by year,
  Trip by trip, hour by hour, moment by moment.

A vista—unsurpassed—
  Not because of its unequaled beauty,
    Though to us it has become that now
  But because of what has happened to those
    Who came to its brow—
    And looked, pondered, imagined,
    Became inspired and moved.

It has distance, breadth, expansion,
  A vista pulling one onward and outward—
  Serenity and hopes unending.

A scene—hundreds of camper eyes have viewed,
  The young, the older, those being led and those leading—
  Thoughts sprung, thoughts deepened,
  Convictions begun and seasoned.

Counselors and campers, adults and staff—
  All, in a sense, humble and equal,
    Different only in background and experience
    And comprehension of its history, beauty and meaning—
    Its place in our lives—in our future—
  All have come to its view.

To those who have seen it—
   Cloud covered, cloudless and clear,
      Sun lit, star lit, moon lit;
      Storm swept, brilliant and loud,
      Drenched with rain, gentle and strong;
      Pastured, planted and harvested;
      Blanketed in sleet with diamond crystalled branch and stem,
      In white—in green—in gold,
      Spring, summer and cold.
   Increasingly captures deeper meaning and importance—
   Our heritage—the birthright of all.

Measurable events have happened here in its full view—
   Discoveries and learnings,
      Campfires, peaceful canvassed slumber,
      Songs, poetry, art—silence and laughter;
         Wild creatures prowling, birds soaring,
         Vegetation tame and wild,
         And people unadjusted but adjusting,
         Young voices of inexperience,
         Others with more maturity—all yielding;
         Yielding to its majesty and powers.

It leads—its messages interpreted through us
   Have been placed in hundreds of souls
      Who have translated its function
      In numerous other places and roles.

It is awe inspiring, spiritually uplifting—
   God created—
May it continue to better persons hew
Our Heart-of-the-Hills View.

Sharp, L. B. (1963). *Heart-of-the-hills view*. [Poem on holiday card].
Carbondale, IL: Outdoor Education Association.

Appendix C

To his Memory

To he, who devoted so much of his life
   to outdoor education,
And, to the world of camping
   gave so many innovations.
He started out with the Life Camps
   back in nineteen twenty-five,
Back when kids were swarmed in barracks
   like bees swarmed in a hive.

He gave to each child initiative
   He tore the barracks down,
Decentralized into small group units,
   Tossed the bugle to the ground.
Here each could taste of the outdoor living.
   Enjoy the fruit of his toil,
Learn to live and work and share with others,
   And learn to love our soil.

He loved the out of doors, the woods;
   To him 'twas food and drink,
In the lonely forest's solitude
   What better place to think.
Amid the splendor of the pines
   What chapel could compare
With this, God's own creative work;
   He walked with reverence there.

He was a dreamer with high ideals
    in a mercenary, work-a-day world;
His ship was launched, put out to sea,
    Its sails outspread, its flag unfurled;
It bravely battled the angry seas.
    The havoc the elements wrought;
Let's sail his ship around the world
    And bring it safely back to port.

To he, who gave so much of his life,
    May his ideals live on and on;
Let the O. E. A. be his monument
    As he journeys in the great beyond.
What greater memorial to L. B. Sharp,
    The battles yet to be won,
Than to carry on with his slogan
    "Not finished, but just begun."

van Dien, M. (1965). To his memory. [Poem]. *The L. B. Sharp Papers*, Morris Library Special Collections, Southern Illinois University, Carbondale, Illinois.

References

Adventures in camping. (1943). New York: Johanna M. Lindlof Camp Committee for Public School Children.

Ambry, E. J. (n.d.) Information on ruling by State Board of Education of New Jersey concerning outdoor education. *The L. B. Sharp Papers*, Morris Library Special Collections, Southern Illinois University, Carbondale, Illinois, Box 29.

Ambry, E. J. (1954). Letter to Wapalanne Friends. *The L. B. Sharp Papers*, Morris Library Special Collections, Southern Illinois University, Carbondale, Illinois, Box 13.

Ambry, E. J. (1960, April 7). Letter to William Freeberg. *The L. B. Sharp Papers*, Morris Library Special Collections, Southern Illinois University, Carbondale, Illinois, Box 29.

Ambry, E. J. (1964, May 4). Letter to Ann Brinley. *The L. B. Sharp Papers*, Morris Library Special Collections, Southern Illinois University, Carbondale, Illinois, Box 29.

Ambry, E. J. & Yambert, P. A. (1972, April 15). *Letter to all friends of L. B. Sharp and registration form.* [Brochure]. Carbondale, IL: Southern Illinois University Outdoor Laboratories.

Area fund drive planned for wilderness classroom. (1964, May 29). *The Southern Illinoisan*, p. 1.

Bass, B. M. (1985). Leadership and performance beyond expectations. New York: Free Press.

Bass, B. M. (1990). From transactional to transformational leadership; Learning to share the vision. *Organizational Dynamics, 18*, 19–31.

Beck, L. (1994). *Reclaiming educational administration as a caring profession.* New York: Teachers College Press.

Beckes, I. K. (1949, October 28). Letter to L. B. Sharp. *The L. B. Sharp Papers*, Morris Library Special Collections, Southern Illinois University, Carbondale, Illinois, Box 11.

Beckett, C. (1963, December 5). Western Union message to the following. *The L. B. Sharp Papers*, Morris Library Special Collections, Southern Illinois University, Carbondale, Illinois, Box 37.

Brennan, M. J. (1962, December 17). Letter to L. B. Sharp. *The L. B. Sharp Papers*, Morris Library Special Collections, Southern Illinois University, Carbondale, Illinois, Box 18.

Brennan, M. J. (1963, March 26). Letter to L. B. Sharp. *The L. B. Sharp Papers*, Morris Library Special Collections, Southern Illinois University, Carbondale, Illinois, Box 18.

Bridges, E. M., & Hallinger, P. (1997). Using problem-based learning to prepare educational leaders. *Peabody Journal of Education*, 72(2), 131–146.

Brinley, A. (1964). Notes for newsletter. *The L. B. Sharp Papers*, Morris Library Special Collections, Southern Illinois University, Carbondale, Illinois, Box 29.

Brinley, A., & Ambry, E. (1963, December). Letter to friends and associates of L. B. Sharp. *The L. B. Sharp Papers*, Morris Library Special Collections, Southern Illinois University, Carbondale, Illinois, Box 37.

Brumbaugh, R. S., & Lawrence, N. M. (1963). *Philosophers on education: Six essays on the foundations of Western thought*. Boston, MA: Houghton Mifflin Co.

Burns, J. M. (1978). *Leadership*. New York: Harper & Row.

Carson, R. (1962). *Silent spring*. New York: Houghton-Mifflin.

Chavez, D. V. (1995). *The status of environmental education in Texas public schools*. Education Service Center, Region X. (Doctoral dissertation. Texas A & M University, College Station, TX).

Clandinin, D. J., & Connelly, F. M. (2000). *Narrative inquiry: Experience and story in qualitative research*. San Francisco: Jossey-Bass.

Conrad, L. H. (1964, May 6). A tribute to Dr. L. B. Sharp. *The L. B. Sharp Papers*, Morris Library Special Collections, Southern Illinois University, Carbondale, Illinois, Box 37.

Conrad, L. H. (1972). Lloyd B. Sharp's philosophy of education. In G. W. Donaldson & O. Goering (Eds.), *Perspectives of outdoor education: Readings* (pp. 16–20). Dubuque, Iowa: Wm. C. Brown Company.

Craft, H. K. (1939, May 17). Letter from Executive Director of the Harlem Branch of the Young Men's Christian Association to L. B. Sharp. *The L. B. Sharp Papers*, Morris Library Special Collections, Southern Illinois University, Carbondale, Illinois, Box 1.

"Death certificate." (1963, December 5). *The L. B. Sharp Papers*, Morris Library Special Collections, Southern Illinois University, Carbondale, Illinois, Box 37.

Dewey, J. (1937, August). In March of Time (Producer), *Youth in camps: Life's Summer Camps* [Film]. (Available from Instructional Support Services, Indiana University, 601 East Kirkwood Avenue, Bloomington, IN 47405-1223)

Dewey, J. (1990). *The school and society. The child and the curriculum*. Chicago: University of Chicago Press. (Original work published in 1900 and 1902, respectively)

Dewey, J. (1997a). *Democracy and education*. New York: Simon & Schuster, Inc. (Original work published in 1916)

Dewey, J. (1997b). *Experience and education*. New York: Touchstone. (Original work published in 1938)

Donaldson, G. W., & Donaldson, L. E. (1982). Whatever happened to school camping? *Camping, 54*(3), 13–20.

Elicker, P. E. (1947). Foreword. *Bulletin of the National Association of Secondary-School Principals, 31*(147), 7.

Elliott, E. B., & Smith, J. W. (1947). The Michigan Program in Action. *Bulletin of the National Association of Secondary-School Principals, 31*(147), 60–74.

Extending Education,1(1). (1944). New York: National Camp of Life Camps, Inc.

Extending Education,6(1). (1961). Carbondale, IL: Outdoor Education Association.

Extending education through camping. (1948). New York: Life Camps, Inc.

Fine, L. J. (1987). Lloyd Burgess Sharp's design criteria for organized residential camps and outdoor centers. (Doctoral dissertation, Southern Illinois University at Carbondale). *University Microfilms International*, 8903688.

Fretwell, E. K. (1943, December 30). Letter to L. B. Sharp. *The L. B. Sharp Papers*, Morris Library Special Collections, Southern Illinois University, Carbondale, Illinois, Box 2.

Gilbert, E. (1898, April 18). Letter to Life Publishing Company. *The L. B. Sharp Papers*, Morris Library Special Collections, Southern Illinois University, Carbondale, Illinois, Box 1.

Gillis, A. (1939, May 1). Letter from Principal of P.S. 3, Brooklyn, New York to Johanna M. Lindlof, Commissioner of Education, New York, New York. *The L. B. Sharp Papers*, Morris Library Special Collections, Southern Illinois University, Carbondale, Illinois, Box 1.

Goodrich, B. F. (1939, November 29). Letter to L. B. Sharp. *The L. B. Sharp Papers*, Morris Library Special Collections, Southern Illinois University, Carbondale, Illinois, Box 1.

Goodrich, L. (1951, November 30). Letter to L. B. Sharp, Bill, and D. Burns. *The L. B. Sharp Papers*, Morris Library Special Collections, Southern Illinois University, Carbondale, Illinois, Box 18.

Goodrich, L. (1953, June 17). Letter to Counselors and Chiefs all down through the years. *The L. B. Sharp Papers*, Morris Library Special Collections, Southern Illinois University, Carbondale, Illinois, Box 18.

Gutek, G. L. (1991). *An historical introduction to American education*. Prospect Heights, IL: Waveland Press.

Hammerman, D. R., & Hammerman, W. M. (1980). Overview. In W. M. Hammerman (Ed.), *Fifty years of resident outdoor education: 1930–1980* (pp. 1–12). Martinsville, IN: American Camping Association.

Hammerman, D. R., Hammerman, W. M., & Hammerman, E. L. (Eds.). (1994). *Teaching in the outdoors* (4th ed.). Danville, IL: Interstate.

Hatch, J. A., & Wisniewski, R. (1995). Life history and narrative: Questions, issues, and exemplary works. In J. A. Hatch & R. Wisniewski (Eds.), *Life history and narrative* (pp. 113–135). London: Falmer Press.

Hickman, L. A. (1998). (Ed.). *Reading Dewey: Interpretations for a postmodern generation*. Bloomington, IN: Indiana University Press.

"John N. Sharp." (1924, June 18). *Carbondale Record*. Osage County, Kansas.

Journal of Outdoor Education, 1(1) (1966). Pilot issue. Dekalb, IL: Northern Illinois University.

Journal of Therapeutic Wilderness Camping. (2004). Procedures for submission of articles. *Journal of Therapeutic Wilderness Camping, 4*(2), 49.

Knapp, C. E. (Ed.). (1991). *The growth of outdoor teacher education: Forty years after the vision*. DeKalb, IL: Northern Illinois University.

Knapp, C. E. (2000). Learning from an outdoor education hero: Personal reflections about L. B. Sharp. *Taproot, 12*(2), 7–11.

Kouzes, J. M., & Posner, B. Z. (2002). *The leadership challenge*. San Francisco: Jossey-Bass.

Land for Learning. (1964). Carbondale, IL: Southern Illinois University and the Outdoor Education Association, Inc.

"Life Camp history pertinent to Camp Raritan." (n.d.). *The L. B. Sharp Papers*, Morris Library Special Collections, Southern Illinois University, Carbondale, Illinois, Box 3.

Life Camps. (1937, July 12). *Time Weekly Magazine, 30*(2), 28.

Life Camps, Inc. (1942). *New Jersey Camping Education Institute Report*. Sussex, NJ: Life Camps, Inc.

Lindenmuth, L. (1964, January 5). Letter to Jean Sticher. *The L. B. Sharp Papers*, Morris Library Special Collections, Southern Illinois University, Carbondale, Illinois, Box 37.

Lindlof, J. M. (1939, December 14). Letter to L. B. Sharp. *The L. B. Sharp Papers*, Morris Library Special Collections, Southern Illinois University, Carbondale, Illinois, Box 1.

"Lloyd B. Sharp ex-Carbondale doctor is dead." (1963, December 6). *Topeka Daily Capitol*, p. 28.

Loughmiller, C. (1947, May 16). Letter to L. B. Sharp. *The L. B. Sharp Papers*, Morris Library Special Collections, Southern Illinois University, Carbondale, Illinois, Box 32.

Loughmiller, C. (1954, February 22). Letter to L. B. Sharp. *The L. B. Sharp Papers*, Morris Library Special Collections, Southern Illinois University, Carbondale, Illinois, Box 29.

Loughmiller, C. (1965). *Wilderness road*. Austin, TX: Hogg Foundation for Mental Health, University of Texas.

Lyons, W. (1961, October 14). Release: Immediate, Southern Illinois University. [Press release]. *The L. B. Sharp Papers*, Morris Library Special Collections, Southern Illinois University, Carbondale, Illinois, Box 18.

March of Time. (Producer). (1937, August). *Youth in camps: Life's Summer Camps* [Film]. (Available from Instructional Support Services, Indiana University, 601 East Kirkwood Avenue, Bloomington, IN 47405-1223)

McCall, M. W., & Lombardo, M. M. (1983). *Off the track: Why and how successful executives get derailed*. Greensboro, NC: Center for Creative Leadership.

Merriam-Webster's collegiate dictionary. 10th ed. (1993). Springfield, MA: Merriam-Webster, Inc.

Mitchell, B. (1988). *Delyte Morris at Southern Illinois University*. Carbondale, IL: Southern Illinois Press.

Mohr, U. O. (1925, April 15). Letter to Assistant Treasurer of Life's Fresh Air Fund. *The L. B. Sharp Papers*, Morris Library Special Collections, Southern Illinois University, Carbondale, Illinois, Box 1.

"Mrs. Emma Sharp dead." (1930, February). *Carbondale Record.* Osage County, Kansas.

Nash, Jay B. (1950, November 30). Letter to L. B. Sharp. *The L. B. Sharp Papers*, Morris Library Special Collections, Southern Illinois University, Carbondale, Illinois, Box 2.

National Camp. (1951). Special session for church camp leaders. [Brochure]. Port Jervis, NY: National Camp. *The L. B. Sharp Papers*, Morris Library Special Collections, Southern Illinois University, Carbondale, Illinois, Box 11.

National Camp. (1958, July, August, September). National training camps. [Brochures]. Port Jervis, NY: National Camp. *The L. B. Sharp Papers*, Morris Library Special Collections, Southern Illinois University, Carbondale, Illinois, Box 11.

National Camp. (1959). National training camps for church camp leaders. [Brochure]. Port Jervis, NY: National Camp. *The L. B. Sharp Papers*, Morris Library Special Collections, Southern Illinois University, Carbondale, Illinois, Box 11.

National Camp. (1961). National and area training camps for church camp leaders. [Brochure]. Port Jervis, NY: National Camp. *The L. B. Sharp Papers*, Morris Library Special Collections, Southern Illinois University, Carbondale, Illinois, Box 11.

"New frontier." (1938, October 17). *Time Weekly Magazine, 32*(16), 39.

New Jersey Outdoor Education Association and the National Outdoor Education Association. (1965). *The L. B. Sharp Memorial Outdoor Education Conference.* [Bulletin]. Branchville, NJ: New Jersey State School of Conservation.

New York University. (1949, July 5–August 12). Lake Sebago Camp Summer Session. [Brochure]. New York: New York University. *The L. B. Sharp Papers*, Morris Library Special Collections, Southern Illinois University, Carbondale, Illinois, Box 2.

Noddings, N. (1992). *The challenge to care in schools.* New York: Teachers College Press.

Northouse, P. G. (2007). *Leadership Theory and Practice* (4th ed.). Thousand Oaks, CA: Sage Publications.

Outdoor Education Association. (n.d.). *Outdoor education* [Brochure]. New York: Outdoor Education Association.

Outdoor Education Association. (1955). Camp Pole Bridge. *The L. B. Sharp Papers*, Morris Library Special Collections, Southern Illinois University, Carbondale, Illinois, Box 13.

Outdoor Education Center opens today at Little Grassy. (1963, October 30). *The Southern Illinoisan*.

Palmer, P. (1993). *To know as we are known: Education as a spiritual journey*. San Francisco: Harper.

Partridge, E. D. (1943). National Camp: Reprint. *Nature Magazine, 36*(6).

Physical education staff meeting. (1932, December 20). Memorandum. *The L. B. Sharp Papers*, Morris Library Special Collections, Southern Illinois University, Carbondale, Illinois, Box 36.

Piercy, I. (1978). The extent of influence of Lloyd Burgess Sharp as identified in the lives and professional careers of selected educators and youth leaders. (Doctoral dissertation, University of Oregon). *University Microfilms International*, 7907494.

Playground and Recreation Association of America. (1924). *Camping out: A manual on organized camping*. New York: MacMillan Company.

Polkinghorne, D. E. (1995). Narrative configuration in qualitative analysis. In J. A. Hatch & R. Wisniewski (Eds.), *Life history and narrative* (pp. 5–23). London: Falmer Press.

Pons, M. (1958, September 1). Introduction of trailer travel camping of Camp Wapalanne. Unpublished manuscript. *The L. B. Sharp Papers*, Morris Library Special Collections, Southern Illinois University, Carbondale, Illinois, Box 13.

Pratt, F. D. (1953, May 18). Letter to Dear Friends of Life Camps. *The L. B. Sharp Papers*, Morris Library Special Collections, Southern Illinois University, Carbondale, Illinois, Box 18.

Regional History Center. (2005). *Lorado Taft Campus. Scope and content*. Northern Illinois University. Retrieved June 22, 2005, from http://www.niulib.niu.edu/reghist/UA%2032.htm#scope

Rettew, D. (1959). Letter to L. B. Sharp. *The L. B. Sharp Papers*, Morris Library Special Collections, Southern Illinois University, Carbondale, Illinois, Box 30.

Rillo, T. (1980a). Contributions of Lloyd B. Sharp. In W. M. Hammerman (Ed.), *Fifty years of resident outdoor education: 1930–1980* (pp. 19–28). Martinsville, IN: American Camping Association.

Rillo, T. (1980b). ACA members contribute significantly. *Camping*, 13.

Rillo, T. J. (1994). Foreword to third edition. In D. R. Hammerman, W. M. Hammerman, & E. L. Hammerman (Eds.), *Teaching in the outdoors* (4th ed.) (pp. xiv–xv). Danville, IL: Interstate Publishers.

Rillo, T. J. (2001). *Education in environmental involvement outdoors*. Tucson, AZ: Safari Club International Foundation.

Ritchie, D. A. (1995). *Doing oral history*. New York: Twayne Publishers.

Rosebrock, A. (1961). The place of the New Jersey State School of Conservation in the outdoor education movement. *Extending Education, 5*(1), 1–2.

"Salute to Cap'n Bill." (1957, November). *American Nature Study Society Newsletter, 1*, 4.

Secretary of Life's Fresh Air Fund. (1925, January 28). Letter to Rev. O. U. Mohr and Mrs. Mohr. *The L. B. Sharp Papers*, Morris Library Special Collections, Southern Illinois University, Carbondale, Illinois, Box 1.

Sergiovanni, T. J. (1996). *Moral leadership: Getting to the heart of school improvement*. San Francisco: Jossey-Bass.

Sergiovanni, T. J. (2006). *Rethinking leadership: A collection of articles* (2nd ed.). Thousand Oaks, CA: Sage Publications.

Sharp, L. B. (1925). Explanation of camp reports. *The L. B. Sharp Papers*, Morris Library Special Collections, Southern Illinois University, Carbondale, Illinois, Box 1.

Sharp, L. B. (1930). *Education and the summer camp: An experiment*. (Doctoral dissertation, Teachers College, Columbia University).

Sharp, L. B. (1935, November 15). Memorandum to Lois Goodrich and Chief Feeley. *The L. B. Sharp Papers*, Morris Library Special Collections, Southern Illinois University, Carbondale, Illinois, Box 1.

Sharp, L. B. (1938). Nature. Life Camps Christmas card of 1938. *The L. B. Sharp Papers*, Morris Library Special Collections, Southern Illinois University, Carbondale, Illinois, Box 1.

Sharp, L. B. (1943a). Outside the classroom. *The Educational Forum*, 7(4), 361–368.

Sharp, L. B. (1943b, March 22). Letter to David Brumbaugh. *The L. B. Sharp Papers*, Morris Library Special Collections, Southern Illinois University, Carbondale, Illinois, Box 36.

Sharp, L. B. (1944). Statement of purpose. *Extending Education*, 1(1), 1.

Sharp, L. B. (1945a, May 23). Letter to Pvt. James M. van Dien, Fort Knox, Kentucky. *The L. B. Sharp Papers*, Morris Library Special Collections, Southern Illinois University, Carbondale, Illinois, Box 30.

Sharp, L. B. (1945b, September 6). Letter to Cap'n Bill (William G. Vinal). *The L. B. Sharp Papers*, Morris Library Special Collections, Southern Illinois University, Carbondale, Illinois, Box 30.

Sharp, L. B. (1946a, February 2–6). *Report of children's camp project, Salesmanship Club of Dallas*. National Camp, Life Camps, Inc.

Sharp, L. B. (1946b, March 20). Conversation with Hugh Masters. Transcript. *The L. B. Sharp Papers*, Morris Library Special Collections, Southern Illinois University, Carbondale, Illinois, Box 30.

Sharp, L. B. (1946c, February 27). Letter to Roy Larsen. *The L. B. Sharp Papers*, Morris Library Special Collections, Southern Illinois University, Carbondale, Illinois, Box 1.

Sharp, L. B. (1947, March 28). Letter to Alice. *The L. B. Sharp Papers*, Morris Library Special Collections, Southern Illinois University, Carbondale, Illinois, Box 2.

Sharp, L. B. (1949a, February). Letter to L. E. Kimble, Vice-Chancellor, New York University. *The L. B. Sharp Papers*, Morris Library Special Collections, Southern Illinois University, Carbondale, Illinois, Box 2.

Sharp, L. B. (1949b, March 11). Letter to C. D. Jackson and Francis Pratt. *The L. B. Sharp Papers*, Morris Library Special Collections, Southern Illinois University, Carbondale, Illinois, Box 2.

Sharp, L. B. (1951a, January 12). Letter to Reynold Carlson. *The L. B. Sharp Papers*, Morris Library Special Collections, Southern Illinois University, Carbondale, Illinois, Box 11.

Sharp, L. B. (1951b, February 27). Letter to Campbell Loughmiller. *The L. B. Sharp Papers*, Morris Library Special Collections, Southern Illinois University, Carbondale, Illinois, Box 11.

Sharp, L. B. (1952). *Survey for Southern Illinois University for development of outdoor education*. New York: Outdoor Education Association.

Sharp, L. B. (1953, December 7). Letter to Julian Smith. *The L. B. Sharp Papers*, Morris Library Special Collections, Southern Illinois University, Carbondale, Illinois, Box 30.

Sharp, L. B. (1957, September 12). Letter to Coswell Miles. *The L. B. Sharp Papers*, Morris Library Special Collections, Southern Illinois University, Carbondale, Illinois, Box 29.

Sharp, L. B. (1959a, February 10). Letter to Don Rettew. *The L. B. Sharp Papers*, Morris Library Special Collections, Southern Illinois University, Carbondale, Illinois, Box 30.

Sharp, L. B. (1959b, October 11). Letter to Bill Goodall. *The L. B. Sharp Papers*, Morris Library Special Collections, Southern Illinois University, Carbondale, Illinois, Box 32.

Sharp, L. B. (1960a). *Administrators, teachers and the out-of-doors*. Address presented at the first National Outdoor Teacher Education conference, Oregon, IL: September 1960.

Sharp, L. B. (1960b, June 24). Letter to Bill Freeberg. *The L. B. Sharp Papers*, Morris Library Special Collections, Southern Illinois University, Carbondale, Illinois, Box 29.

Sharp, L. B. (1961a). SIBOGI Outdoor Education Center for Southern Illinois University at Little Grassy Lake survey and master plan. Carbondale, IL: Southern Illinois University. *The L. B. Sharp Papers*, Morris Library Special Collections, Southern Illinois University, Carbondale, Illinois, Box 18.

Sharp, L. B. (1961b, October 6). Letter to Russ and Helena Rayner. *The L. B. Sharp Papers*, Morris Library Special Collections, Southern Illinois University, Carbondale, Illinois, Box 13.

Sharp, L. B. (1961c, October 9). Letter to Pole Bridge staff members. *The L. B. Sharp Papers*, Morris Library Special Collections, Southern Illinois University, Carbondale, Illinois, Box 13.

Sharp, L. B. (1961d, October 9). Letter to Pole Bridge campers and parents. *The L. B. Sharp Papers*, Morris Library Special Collections, Southern Illinois University, Carbondale, Illinois, Box 18.

Sharp, L. B. (1962, December 20). Letter to Matthew Brennan. *The L. B. Sharp Papers*, Morris Library Special Collections, Southern Illinois University, Carbondale, Illinois, Box 18.

Sharp, L. B. (1963a, July 25). Letter to Rev. Rodney Britten. *The L. B. Sharp Papers*, Morris Library Special Collections, Southern Illinois University, Carbondale, Illinois, Box 29.

Sharp, L. B. (1963b, April 16). Letter to Edward Ambry. *The L. B. Sharp Papers*, Morris Library Special Collections, Southern Illinois University, Carbondale, Illinois, Box 29.

Sharp, L. B. (1963c, July 27). Letter to Edward Ambry and Thomas Rillo. *The L. B. Sharp Papers*, Morris Library Special Collections, Southern Illinois University, Carbondale, Illinois, Box 29.

Sharp, L. B. (1963d, October 11). Letter to C. D. Jackson. *The L. B. Sharp Papers*, Morris Library Special Collections, Southern Illinois University, Carbondale, Illinois, Box 29.

Smith, J. W. (1947, March 26). Letter to Dr. L. B. Sharp. *The L. B. Sharp Papers*, Morris Library Special Collections, Southern Illinois University, Carbondale, Illinois, Box 32.

Smith, J. W. (1955, October 11). Letter to L. B. Sharp. *The L. B. Sharp Papers*, Morris Library Special Collections, Southern Illinois University, Carbondale, Illinois, Box 30.

Smith, J. W. (1973). Where we have been, what we are, what we will become: The Taft Campus Outdoor Education Award Lecture, 1970. In D. R. Hammerman & W. M. Hammerman (Eds.), *Outdoor education: A book of readings* (2nd ed., pp. 48–54). Minneapolis, MN: Burgess.

Southern Illinois University. (2002). *Touch of Nature area overview*. [Brochure]. Carbondale, IL: Southern Illinois University.

Stewart, J. (2006). Transformational leadership: An evolving concept examined through the works of Burns, Bass, Avolio, and Leithwood. *Canadian Journal of Educational Administration and Policy, 54*. Retrieved October 20, 2007, from http://vnweb.hwwilsonweb.com/hww/jumpstart.jhtml

Stogdill, R. (1974). *Handbook of leadership: A survey of the literature*. New York: The Free Press.

Strauss, A., & Corbin, J. (1998). *Basics of qualitative research* (2nd ed.). Thousand Oaks, CA: Sage Publishers.

Taylor, L. E. (n. d.). *L. B. Sharp in memorandum*. Held in the private collection of Clifford E. Knapp.

Taylor, L. E. (1963, October 29) Letter to Don Hammerman. *The L. B. Sharp Papers*, Morris Library Special Collections, Southern Illinois University, Carbondale, Illinois, Box 29.

The L. B. Sharp Papers. (2002, February). *The L. B. Sharp Papers*, Morris Library Special Collections, Southern Illinois University, Carbondale, Illinois, Box 36.

Time, Inc. (1944, September 28). [Memo]. Time, Inc. program for Life Camp, Inc. *The L. B. Sharp Papers*, Morris Library Special Collections, Southern Illinois University, Carbondale, Illinois, Box 1.

Treu, J. (1947). What is the night? *Bulletin of the National Association of Secondary-School Principals, 31*(147), 93.

van Dien, M. (1965). To his memory. *The L. B. Sharp Papers*, Morris Library Special Collections, Southern Illinois University, Carbondale, Illinois, Box 37.

Vinal, W. G. (1944). Vesper services in camp. Reprint from March 1944 *Camping* Magazine. *The L. B. Sharp Papers*, Morris Library Special Collections, Southern Illinois University, Carbondale, Illinois, Box 18.

Vinal, W. G. (1945). Letter to L. B. Sharp. *The L. B. Sharp Papers*, Morris Library Special Collections, Southern Illinois University, Carbondale, Illinois, Box 30.

Vinal, W. G. (1972). Still more outdoor leaders I have known. In G. W. Donaldson & O. Goering (Eds.), *Perspectives of outdoor education: Readings* (pp. 45–49). Dubuque, Iowa: Wm. C. Brown Company.

Walker, P. C. (1953, May 18). Letter to L. B. Sharp. *The L. B. Sharp Papers*, Morris Library Special Collections, Southern Illinois University, Carbondale, Illinois, Box 18.

Wiener, M. (1965). Developing a rationale for outdoor education. (Doctoral dissertation, Michigan State University). *University Microfilms International*, 65-14290.

Willis, W. W. (1963, December 5). Letter to Mrs. Herman Barkmann. *The L. B. Sharp Papers*, Morris Library Special Collections, Southern Illinois University, Carbondale, Illinois, Box 37.

Wisconsin vital records indexes. (2002, April 15). Pre-1907 Birth Index. Alice Whitney, Reel 0320, Record DX0604.

Yale Club. (1938, April 5). Transcripts from interview with L. B. Sharp by Luce, Dwyer, Blankenhorn, and Hurst, Yale Club, New York City. *The L. B. Sharp Papers*, Morris Library Special Collections, Southern Illinois University, Carbondale, Illinois, Box 18.